AGENTS OF CHANGE
Internal Auditors in an Era of Disruption

Best wishes!

Richard F. Chambers

Sponsored by
AUDITBOARD

INTERNAL AUDIT
FOUNDATION

"They say timing is everything, and that is certainly the case for Richard Chambers' latest book. *Agents of Change* brings a vital message about the transformational change needed in internal auditing at a time when organizations are reeling from dramatic and dynamic change. The magnanimous wisdom of Richard, combined with his talented co-author Robert Pérez, offer a compelling and inspiring challenge for practitioners to become catalysts for change in their organizations, together with a concise and insightful blueprint for how to get it done. Bravo!"

Jenitha John, CIA, QIAL
CEO, Independent Regulatory Board of Auditors
South Africa

"Another masterpiece from Richard! Each page turned revealed more nuggets of insight that will enable all auditors to become Agents of Change, influencing positive change that enhances our organisation's value. This book is an essential element of any auditor's toolkit!"

David Hill, CIA, CMIIA, QIAL
Chief Executive Officer
SWAP Internal Audit Services

"As we race toward the inevitable convergence of several disruptive technologies, Richard Chambers' timely book highlights the imperative that internal auditors must be ready for the future. He correctly points out that to add value to the organization, internal auditors must lead by example and be agents of change."

Charlie Wright, CIA, CPA, CISA
Chief Risk Officer
Jack Henry and Associates

"Once again, in a hat trick, Richard has produced a treatise of wisdom for internal auditors, gleaned from his decades of experience, crystal clear thinking, and piercing focus on the future. *Agents of Change: Internal Auditors in an Era of Disruption* is an outstanding guide for all internal auditors to plan their trajectories to become 'catalysts for transformation' and enhance value for their organizations. Richard highlights the skillsets and the mindset needed by internal auditors to change their DNA in preparation for the future. Most importantly, he advocates that the profession, going forward, not merely has to highlight risks facing our organizations but also identify opportunities for growth and improvement. In short, this is a survival guide. Internal auditors, ignore this book and your organizations will ignore you!"

Naren Aneja
Founder and Chief Executive
Aneja Associates
(International Internal Auditors)

"In *Agents of Change,* Richard has written an intuitive and in-depth perspective of the role of the internal audit function at present and well into the future. Sound guidance from a respected global leader in the internal audit profession. Read this book and learn from one of the best!"

Mike Cowell
Executive Vice President, Chief Auditor
TIAA

"My professional acquaintance with Richard Chambers dates back more than two decades, and over that time he has been a consistent source of insights and vision about the evolving role of internal audit. In his latest book, Richard's passion for the profession comes through and lights the way for the next evolution in internal auditing. *Agents of Change: Internal Auditors in an Era of Disruption* is a must-read for anyone who wishes to understand the interplay of risk, technology, business, and the constancy of change."

> Ellen Caya
> Chief Audit Executive and Corp. VP-Global Internal Audit
> McDonald's Corporation

"A very timely call for action for all internal auditors in the age of disruption! From internal auditors changing themselves to becoming catalysts of change, Richard shares a wealth of insight and wisdom on what it takes for internal auditors to drive value for the organizations they serve."

> Prof. Bao Guoming, CIA
> Chair
> China Institute of Internal Audit (IIA–China)

"Every single chapter of Richard's previous books offered some insightful takeaway or message. This latest book not only does the same but also inspires internal auditors to take a lead in meaningful and transformational change to positively impact their organizations."

> J. Michael Peppers, CIA, QIAL, CRMA, CPA
> Chief Audit Executive
> The University of Texas System

"Richard Chambers has been at the forefront in moving the audit profession forward. *Agents of Change* builds off the concepts in *Lessons Learned on the Audit Trail* and *Trusted Advisors* and will inspire internal auditors and risk professionals of all levels to boldly be catalysts for change in our organizations."

> Seth Peterson, CIA, QIAL, CRMA, CISA
> Chief Enterprise Risk Assurance Executive
> The First National Bank in Sioux Falls

"Richard Chambers shares key insights on how internal auditors can become change agents by not only providing objective assurance, advice, and insights but how to be influential, add value, and be instrumental in helping their organizations be successful. Stakeholder expectations are high for internal audit to be agile, innovative, to have business acumen, to leverage technology, and to be an agent of change! A must-read for leaders at all levels who want to make a difference in their organizations."

> Sandy Pundmann, CIA, CRMA, CPA
> Global Internal Audit, Senior Partner
> Deloitte & Touche LLP

Copyright © 2021 by Richard F. Chambers. All rights reserved.

Published by the Internal Audit Foundation
1035 Greenwood Blvd., Suite 149
Lake Mary, Florida 32746, USA

No part of this publication may be reproduced, stored in a retrieval system, or transmitted in any form by any means — electronic, mechanical, photocopying, recording, or otherwise — without prior written permission of the publisher. Requests to the publisher for permission should be sent electronically to: copyright@theiia.org with the subject line "reprint permission request."

Limit of Liability: The Internal Audit Foundation publishes this document for informational and educational purposes and is not a substitute for legal or accounting advice. The Foundation does not provide such advice and makes no warranty as to any legal or accounting results through its publication of this document. When legal or accounting issues arise, professional assistance should be sought and retained.

The IIA's International Professional Practices Framework (IPPF) comprises the full range of existing and developing practice guidance for the profession. The IPPF provides guidance to internal auditors globally and paves the way to world-class internal auditing.

The IIA and the Foundation work in partnership with researchers from around the globe who conduct valuable studies on critical issues affecting today's business world. Much of the content presented in their final reports is a result of Foundation-funded research and prepared as a service to the Foundation and the internal audit profession. Expressed opinions, interpretations, or points of view represent a consensus of the researchers and do not necessarily reflect or represent the official position or policies of The IIA or the Foundation.

ISBN-13: 978-1-63454-119-0
25 24 23 22 21   2 3 4 5

Contents

Foreword	xi
Acknowledgments	xv
About the Authors	xvii
Introduction	xix
What Is an Agent of Change?	xx
Trusted Advisors versus Change Agents	xxi
PART ONE: A LEGACY OF CHANGE	**1**
Chapter 1: An Evolving Profession	**3**
The Evolution of Internal Audit	5
The Birth of Independent Audit	6
The Birth of The IIA	7
The Influences of a Dynamic Risk Landscape	9
A Natural Evolution	11
Chapter 2: The Imperative for Change	**13**
Where Internal Audit Is Lagging	14
Outdated Processes	15
What Can We Do About It?	21
Next Steps	23
Chapter 3: Independence Doesn't Imply Isolation	**25**
Independence and Objectivity	29
Maintaining Independence and Objectivity as an Agent of Change	31
The Three Lines Model	32
How We See Ourselves	34
Key Characteristics of Change Agents	35
Hearing from the Change Agents	38
Personal Attributes: Nurture or Nature?	39
Trusted Advisors versus Agents of Change	40

PART TWO: ENACTING THE CHANGE 41

Chapter 4: Agent Change Thyself 43
Appetite for Change 44
Four Areas in Need of Change 45
Developing a Culture of Change............................... 52

Chapter 5: Driving Change Means Being Agile................... 55
A Case Study in Agility... 56
Agile Auditing... 59
Features of Agile Auditing..................................... 61
The Benefits of Agile Auditing 63
The Future of Agile Auditing................................... 64

Chapter 6: Leveraging Enabling Technology...................... 65
Staying the Course: Is It Worth It? 66
Using Technology to Reengineer Internal Audit Processes 68
Audit Management Software Helps Add Value.................. 68
Technology Is Essential to Agility............................. 70
Data Analytics Help Auditors Know Their Business 70
Employing Emerging Technologies Is Crucial to
   Leading Change 71
Integrated Risk Management: The Key to Building Strong
   Relationships.. 72
Creating Time Is Creating Value................................ 73
How to Begin Building a Change-Enabling Foundation.......... 73

Chapter 7: Agents of Change Aren't Secret Agents................ 77
Recasting the Internal Audit Story 78
Is Indispensable Within Reach? 78
Forging an Effective Communication Strategy.................. 82
Formally Updating Our Story................................... 83
Communication and Marketing................................. 86
The Humble Internal Auditor 87
Promoting and Provoking Change.............................. 89

PART THREE: THE RIGHT STUFF.............................	**91**
Chapter 8: Business Acumen	**93**
General Business Acumen...................................	96
Know Your Business..	100
The Change Agent Value Proposition	102
Chapter 9 : The Strategic Internal Auditor......................	**107**
Being Strategic Starts at Home	108
Attributes of Strategic Internal Auditors	110
Avoiding the Pitfalls of Being a Tactical Internal Auditor..........	113
Strategic Internal Auditors and Transformational Change.........	115
Chapter 10: On Being Relationship Centric	**119**
Adding to the Ranks of Change Agents.......................	124
Reaching Beyond Trusted Advisor...........................	125
The Independence Trap	128
Independence Does Not Mean Isolation	131
Chapter 11: The Innovative Mindset............................	**133**
Prepare Yourself for Innovation	134
Learning to Innovate.......................................	138
Why Innovation for Internal Audit?...........................	141
A Final Thought on Innovation	142
Conclusion: Agents of the Future	**143**
Revolutionary Evolution	144
Agents of Change Are Among Us............................	145
Remaining True to the Profession	146
The Constancy of Change	147
Notes	149

List of Exhibits

Exhibit 3-1: 2 in 10 CAEs Operate as Agents of Change 35
Exhibit 3-2: Half of Internal Audit Functions Viewed as
    Change Agents. 36
Exhibit 3-3: Key Attributes of Change Agents 36
Exhibit 3-4: Categories and Rankings of Key Attributes. 37

Exhibit 4-1: Stakeholder Support for Change Agents 51
Exhibit 4-2: Few Internal Audit Functions Viewed as Agents
    of Change 52

Exhibit 7-1: Assurance Conversation 79
Exhibit 7-2: Organizational Relevance 80

Exhibit 8-1: Key Attributes of Change Agents 95
Exhibit 8-2: Skills Categories 98
Exhibit 8-3: Value Proposition 103
Exhibit 8-4: Ascending to the Level of Trusted Advisor. 105
Exhibit 8-5: Ascending to the Level of Agent of Change 105

Exhibit 10-1: 2 in 10 CAEs Operate as Agents of Change 125

*To the men and women of
The Institute of Internal Auditors Global Headquarters.
Their tireless dedication as agents of change
has inspired internal auditors and
elevated the profession for 80 years!*

Foreword

Richard does it again!

It is no secret that Richard's books are popular around the world. Internal audit fans typically queue up in long lines at his speaking engagements to get the latest signed copy and perhaps a quick photo. And Richard doesn't disappoint in *Agents of Change: Internal Auditors in an Era of Disruption*, the final installment in his outstanding trilogy exploring the characteristics of the best of the best and what we should all aspire to be in our profession.

Like his previous books, *Agents of Change* is well-timed as the world copes with a global pandemic and forces us to drastically change how we live, work, and even play. We are certainly living in a time of uncertainty as we pivot to respond to unexpected risks and try to accurately predict what may lie ahead, especially in the very near future. As Richard acknowledges, the only constant in this world is change, which helps him build his case in these pages for why we all must strive to become agents of change — to thrive or, perhaps, simply survive.

When I consider the concept of an agent of change, I cannot think of anyone who fits the description better than Richard. From the time he worked in the U.S. Army to change their audit process to his role as the leading voice, president, and CEO of The IIA, he has consistently demonstrated an ability and zeal to constantly evolve and offer ways to modernize internal auditing so that we can remain relevant to the organizations we work so hard to serve. Through his earlier books, *Lessons Learned on the Audit Trail* (both the first and second editions) and *Trusted Advisors: Key Attributes of Outstanding Internal Auditors*, we had the opportunity to read about Richard's first-hand experiences, learn what he learned over more than 40 years in the profession, and set an informed path toward becoming better at what we do.

He has an impressive track record for meeting challenges head on, defining the opportunities in each situation, and exceeding the expectations of even the most critical among us. He came to The IIA at a time of great turmoil, with the Great

Recession leaving its mark on every organization. It was Richard's time, and he led The IIA from the depths of its worst crisis since the organization was founded in 1941 to achieve exponential growth in membership and certifications. I was fortunate to be part of The IIA's Executive Committee that selected him as our new president and CEO. Richard skillfully navigated The IIA out of dangerous waters with swift, thoughtful, and sometimes radical change. Some of it was painful, but he was determined to do nothing short of saving The IIA and the profession.

Today, The IIA marks record membership and professional certifications, including the flagship Certified Internal Auditor (CIA), in every corner of the world. He did that by embracing innovation, including new technology, and seizing pent-up demand for IIA offerings. As an example, the CIA designation has attracted tens of thousands of internal auditors in recent years after The IIA converted to computer-based exams and opened the certification process to a vastly larger pool of qualified applicants.

Richard continues to amaze with his passion and eagerness to advance our profession. I am not sure how he finds the time to give presentations, write blogs, books, and articles, and represent our profession with various stakeholders such as government and media — all while managing a huge association of more than 110 affiliated organizations globally. But as many who have experienced one of his in-person presentations know, he always takes the time for members and affiliates when they need his help and advice. He is literally walking the talk of the characteristics of an agent of change.

This book is full of practical suggestions that are useful to any auditor who wishes to become an agent of change. Richard's vast knowledge and experience — and recommendations on how to apply his advice in day-to-day activities — add up to a recipe for success. I personally subscribe to everything he suggests in this book. In fact, I tell my team at AIG that "the only constant thing in this life is change, and they will change you if you cannot change." I also tell them that we need to continue to learn and adopt new ways of auditing as our stakeholders' expectations continue to evolve. As this book suggests, we all risk becoming irrelevant amid an ever-disruptive, risk-packed environment.

Richard is direct in addressing the stark reality for those who merely hide behind independence and objectivity, which may make some readers feel uncomfortable. But if you want to be relevant and involved in helping your organization succeed, I encourage you to follow his advice and implement what he suggests. I guarantee you will not regret it, and you will thank Richard for suggesting that you take the risk.

Richard is stepping down as president and CEO of The IIA after 12 rewarding years. I am not sure what the future holds for him and his lovely wife, Kim, but my hope is that we will continue to benefit from his deep and profound knowledge and experience in the profession. He will most likely change the definition of "retirement" as an agent of change. 😊

Naohiro Mouri, CIA, CPA
Executive Vice President and Chief Auditor
American International Group Inc.
IIA Global Chairman, 2018–2019

Acknowledgments

Writing this book has been another rewarding experience in my journey to inform and inspire the global profession of internal auditing. This is the third manuscript I have published, and once again, it would not have been possible without the encouragement and support of so many family members, friends, and colleagues.

I must first acknowledge the extraordinary efforts of my writing partner, Robert Pérez. His vision, energy, and tireless dedication to this project were critical to its success. Robert has been helping me find my voice in my articles, blogs, and books since joining The IIA in 2014. He was the first person I asked to assist me with this book, and I will be eternally grateful that he said yes.

My wife, Kim, has been a vital partner who has been inspiring me to be a change agent for more than 30 years. She is a source of encouragement and support each time I write a book. Her words of advice, reassurance, patience, and understanding were vital to undertaking such demanding projects. My talented and beautiful daughters, Natalie McElwee, Christina Morton, and Allison Chambers, have always been unwavering in their affection and support. As I grow older, I am also motivated by my three grandchildren, Kennedy, MacKenzie, and Luke. They help me maintain a healthy perspective on life.

Thank you to AuditBoard, Inc., for sponsoring this Internal Audit Foundation publication and for their assistance in preparing chapter 6, "Leveraging Enabling Technology." Thanks to Erika Beard and Carrie Summerlin, whose persistence convinced me to write another book for the Internal Audit Foundation. Thanks to John Babinchak and Matthew Bennett for their help in keeping me organized and focused during the many months that this project was under development. Thanks to Harold Silverman, Tim Berichon, Greg Jaynes, and Jim Pelletier for their support and insights during the research and writing phases. Thanks to Ben Bouchillon and Lee Ann Campbell for their contributions in managing this project and putting the finishing touches on the manuscript. Thank you to Monica

Griffin, Jim Kinder, and Maggie Dunn for their extraordinary work on the cover design of the book. Thanks also to Naohiro Mouri for the kind words he shared in the foreword to this edition.

As this will be the last book I will write as president and CEO of The IIA, I would be remiss if I failed to thank all of the men and women in volunteer leadership roles during my years of service who have modeled the change agent attributes explored in this book. I am particularly grateful for the unwavering support I have received from the 13 men and women who chaired The IIA's Board of Directors during my 12-year tenure: Patty Miller, 2008–2009; Rod Winters, 2009–2010; Gunther Meggeneder, 2010–2011; Denny Beran, 2011–2012; Phil Tarling, 2012–2013; Paul Sobel, 2013–2014; Anton van Wyk, 2014–2015; Larry Harrington, 2015–2016; Angela Witzany, 2016–2017; Mike Peppers, 2017–2018; Naohiro Mouri (Mouri-san), 2018–2019; Mike Joyce, 2019–2020; and Jenitha John, 2020–2021.

About the Authors

Richard F. Chambers, CIA, QIAL, CGAP, CCSA, CRMA, is one of the leading voices and thought leaders in the internal audit profession. He has spent more than 40 years in internal audit and association management, including serving as president and CEO of The Institute of Internal Auditors (IIA) from 2009 to 2021. During his tenure at The IIA, he led the organization to achieve record membership while presiding over the launch of numerous key initiatives and achieving key milestones in certifications.

Prior to leading The IIA, Richard was national practice leader in Internal Audit Advisory Services at PwC; inspector general of the Tennessee Valley Authority; deputy inspector general of the U.S. Postal Service; and director of the U.S. Army Worldwide Internal Review Organization at the Pentagon.

A prolific blogger and highly sought-after speaker, Richard has authored two award-winning books: *Trusted Advisors: Key Attributes of Outstanding Internal Auditors* (2017) and *Lessons Learned on the Audit Trail* (2014), which is currently available in five languages. His third book, *The Speed of Risk: Lessons Learned on the Audit Trail,* 2nd Edition, was released in 2019. He has been consistently listed among the 100 Most Influential People in Accounting by *Accounting Today*, and among the most influential leaders in corporate governance by the National Association of Corporate Directors.

Richard and his wife, Kim, reside in New Smyrna Beach, Florida, and have three grown daughters, Natalie, Christina, and Allison.

Robert Pérez is an award-winning writer who has spent nearly four decades as a professional journalist, editor, and strategic communicator. In his current role as The IIA's director of content development and delivery, Robert helps shape communication strategy and thought leadership to support internal audit practitioners globally. He is part of IIA teams that produce the annual *North American Pulse of Internal Audit* report, *OnRisk* guide, and the American Corporate Governance Index.

Prior to joining The IIA in 2014, Robert was vice president of CBR Public Relations. Earlier in his career, he spent more than 25 years as a journalist at several newspapers, including the *Orlando Sentinel*, the *Dallas Times Herald*, and *The Wall Street Journal*.

Robert and his wife, Barbara, reside in the Orlando, Florida, area.

Introduction

When I began contemplating my third book, the intent was to create the final installment of a trilogy.

My first book, *Lessons Learned on the Audit Trail*, was a semi-autobiographical look at my experiences over nearly 40 years in the internal audit profession. I wanted to impart a bit of wisdom based on my exposure to hundreds, if not thousands, of audits and internal auditors who shaped my views of risk, independent assurance, good governance, and the value that internal audit provides. Five years later, I offered an updated look at the audit trail in a second edition to the original manuscript, titled *The Speed of Risk*.

One of the chapters in *Lessons Learned on the Audit Trail* touched on becoming a trusted advisor. I have long preached the value of building relationships with our stakeholders — on the board, in the C-suite, and across the organization — to help elevate internal audit and earn a seat at the table with management and others. This is possible only by demonstrating conclusively and consistently how internal audit helps an organization achieve its goals. The abbreviated examination of some key characteristics of proven trusted advisors provided the genesis for my second book.

For *Trusted Advisors: Key Attributes of Outstanding Internal Auditors*, I surveyed and interviewed an array of leading internal auditors. From those discussions, I gleaned insights into the traits that characterize outstanding internal auditors — those individuals who have earned that seat at the table and are also considered trusted advisors in their organizations. I examined attributes including ethical resiliency, critical thinking, business acumen, intellectual curiosity, dynamic communication skills, and insightful relationship building.

While *Lessons Learned on the Audit Trail* was a retrospective on our roles as assurance and advisory providers, *Trusted Advisors* was a contemporary look at the profession and the traits that leading internal auditors demonstrate in building and sustaining trust. While exploring the past and the present is important, we will never realize our full potential until we look forward. That is where this book, *Agents of Change: Internal Auditors in an Era of Disruption*, is intended to take readers.

What Is an Agent of Change?

My intent is for this book to be a call to action for internal audit practitioners at all levels. To truly impart value to our organizations, we must be catalysts for transformation that creates value within the organizations we serve. To be sure, we add value when our assurance engagements identify corrective measures that need to be undertaken in the wake of audit findings. We certainly add value when we impart advice as our organizations' trusted advisors. But our objectives should not be limited to providing assurance and advice. More importantly, we should be influencing positive change that enhances our organizations' value.

I first wrote about internal auditors as agents of change in a 2015 blog post. In the years since, I have often urged internal auditors to embrace the role and join other catalysts in their organizations who thrive on change and innovation. We have a unique seat at our organizations' table. It is often a seat that affords a 360-degree view of the risks and opportunities facing our stakeholders. We have become adept at highlighting the risks. We must become equally comfortable shining a light on opportunities.

In preparing to write this book, I embraced the same approach I used when writing *Trusted Advisors*. I had my own ideas on how internal auditors can drive change and what it takes to be successful. But I didn't want this book to reflect only my point of view. So, once again, I went to the most reliable source of knowledge of what agents of change are all about — change agents themselves. Working with the Internal Audit Foundation, we surveyed almost 600 chief audit executives (CAEs) and internal audit directors around the world on what it takes to be an agent of change in twenty-first century internal auditing. The results were revealing and provided the basis for this book.

As we did for *Trusted Advisors*, we followed up our survey with in-depth conversations with CAEs who clearly model what it takes to be agents of change. The survey feedback and interviews were very instructive in organizing this book. *Agents of Change* comprises three parts that make the case for becoming change agents, emphasize that internal auditors must start by changing themselves, and articulate the skills embedded in change agents' DNA. Specifically:

PART ONE: A LEGACY OF CHANGE

Modern internal auditors are a product of centuries of change. Indeed, the profession has been in constant evolution since its inception. In the twenty-first century, the velocity of risk has accelerated exponentially, and change can no longer happen at a methodical pace. Indeed, our organizations need us to audit at the speed of risk. The internal audit profession has embraced a vision that it will be indispensable in protecting and enhancing value in the organizations we serve. Those who succeed are the change agents among us.

PART TWO: ENACTING THE CHANGE

Before internal auditors can be indispensable agents of change within our organizations, we must change ourselves. We can no longer embrace processes rooted in the past century if we are to be taken seriously by those we serve in this one. We must bring an agile mindset to the way we execute our mission so that we are truly adept at auditing at the speed of risk. Perhaps most importantly, we must become adept at telling our story. We cannot expect others to envision our potential if we keep our heads down and mouths shut.

PART THREE: THE RIGHT STUFF

The most valuable insights from our global survey were the feedback on the common characteristics of agents of change. Respondents rated the importance of 14 characteristics, and we identified four common traits that distinguish great change agents from the rest. First, they possess strong business acumen and have a keen understanding of their organizations. Second, they bring a strategic mindset to everything they do. Third, strong agents of change are relationship-centric. They recognize that the success in influencing and inspiring change must be rooted in strong, resilient relationships. Fourth, agents of change are innovative. They aren't content with recycling the same solutions. They are purveyors of solutions that drive change and enhance organizational value.

Trusted Advisors versus Change Agents

By now you may be wondering — what is the difference between a trusted advisor and an agent of change? By my definitions, it is not an either/or proposition. Trusted advisors build and sustain trust in those they serve, and the recommendations and advice they offer are valued and embraced by their stakeholders. As I noted earlier, agents of change are catalysts for transformation that creates value within their organizations. They also must be trusted advisors, but not all trusted advisors are agents of change. Trusted advisors are often fulfilled by being heard, while agents of change are fulfilled by inspiring transformation that enhances value.

Internal auditors used to be derisively referred to as "bean counters." The classic assurance providers in the profession still count the beans. Trusted advisors, on the other hand, know how to grow, harvest, and take the beans to market. But it is the change agents in the profession who are bold and confident enough to advocate changing the crops from growing beans to growing corn.

I hope this book will inform and inspire you to become a catalyst for transformation within your organization.

PART ONE

A LEGACY OF CHANGE

CHAPTER 1
An Evolving Profession

— • • • • —

It is not the strongest of the species that survive, nor the most intelligent, but the one most responsive to change.

— Charles Darwin —

I am often asked for the one piece of advice I would give to someone new to the internal audit profession. The answer has been the same for almost two decades: Follow the risks. My reasoning is that we add the greatest value to our organizations when we allocate our scarce, highly skilled talents to the most significant risks — the events that can potentially disrupt or prevent our organizations from attaining their objectives.

It is easy enough to simply say "follow the risks." But it is critically important for internal auditors to understand how risk influences strategies and decisions that executive management and boards make to create and sustain value in our organizations.

These components should feed our understanding of risk, our biases about how risks should be managed, and our views on how internal audit can provide value to organizations. But even as these factors complicate an already unimaginably complex web of risks that affect today's organizations, the work of internal audit comes down to a simple truth first articulated in *La Logique ou l'Art de Penser* (*Logic, or the Art of Thinking*), published in 1662:

> "Fear of harm ought to be proportional not merely to the gravity of the harm but also to the probability of the event."

This is a fundamental concept in risk management — balancing impact and likelihood. Yet, while the work of modern internal auditing is all about risk, we spend surprisingly little time trying to understand our relationship with it, though that relationship is as old as humankind itself.

As long as humans have existed, we have had to manage risk — so much so that risk is embedded in our DNA. I refer to the "fight-or-flight" response built into our brains to handle a perceived or real threat. However, outside of this instinctive response, humans have developed a more sophisticated relationship with risk, one that is built on calculating probabilities and potential rewards. Peter L. Bernstein notes in his 1996 book, *Against the Gods: The Remarkable Story of Risk*, that the word risk derives from the early Italian word risicare, which actually means "to dare." He writes:

> "In this sense, risk is a choice rather than a fate. The actions we dare to take, which depend on how free we are to make choices, are what the story of risk is all about. And that story helps define what it means to be a human being."[1]

This choice to dare is at the heart of modern business theory and something all internal auditors must understand and embrace. The risk/reward concept takes on many forms, from racecar drivers who pit their skills against the risk of serious injury or death to businesses that invest in developing new products or venture into new markets to boost sales and profits.

From an organizational perspective, effectively managing risk — whether external or self-imposed — is fundamental to good governance. What's more, the assurance that an independent and objective internal audit function provides over the effectiveness of risk management is a critical component of sound governance.

While "follow the risk" is the most common piece of advice I give internal auditors, the second most frequent is "adapt to meet the needs and expectations of stakeholders." In fact, "adapting" has been a common theme throughout the history of our profession. Internal auditing in the twenty-first century bears little resemblance to the profession in its early origins. The value being delivered by the profession today is the product of a legacy of change dating back centuries.

The Evolution of Internal Audit

That I have dedicated the first chapters of this book to a discussion on risk is remarkable. The very concept that internal auditors should focus their work on the basis of risk is a relatively recent phenomenon. Not until 2002 did professional standards even mandate a risk assessment in audit planning. But the truth is that the internal audit profession has a legacy of change dating back to its origins.

Any examination of internal auditing in an era of disruption, such as the one in which it finds itself today, requires context and must begin with a review of the profession's history. Understanding how we came to where we are affords an opportunity to analyze significant developments that shaped our thinking, our biases, and our blind spots.

The Institute of Internal Auditors (IIA) has published a number of accounts on the history of internal auditing. Most tend to focus on the organization as much as the profession. I believe that is appropriate in that The IIA is unquestionably the leading voice for the profession and provider of standards, guidance, research, and thought leadership. However, the seeds of internal auditing were planted well before The IIA's founding in 1941.

A friend of mine, University of Dayton Associate Professor Sridhar Ramamoorti, authored an insightful paper, *Internal Auditing: History, Evolution, and Prospects*, published by The IIA's Internal Audit Foundation in 2003.[2] He chronicles events and practices driven by the need for accountability in business and government as far back as 4000 B.C.

Of significance in Ramamoorti's analysis is the evolution of the profession by the early twentieth century and the recognition among stakeholders that the value of assurance went "far beyond financial statement auditing and devoted to furnishing reliable operating reports containing nonfinancial data. . ." This is the earliest acknowledgment that internal audit generates value as a provider of true enterprisewide assurance, and reflects the need for, and willingness of, the profession to change to meet the evolving needs of the organizations it serves.

The value of enterprisewide assurance continues to vex our profession. Few would argue against the vital need for assurance across the enterprise, but there remains disagreement over how it should be delivered — and by whom.

From a historical perspective, the primary risks that drove creation of the need for checks and balances and for controls that predated internal audit revolved around threats to organizational assets. Protecting against losses was the principal driver for creating internal auditing. As Ramamoorti notes:

> "Starting as an internal business function primarily focused on protection against payroll fraud, loss of cash, and other assets, internal audit's scope was quickly extended to the verification of almost all financial transactions . . . (Reeve, 1986)."

It was only later that organizations grasped the value of understanding and managing interrelated risks across the enterprise that encompass not only financial considerations but also those involving compliance, operations, business continuity, culture, and more.

The Birth of Independent Audit

Studies of the evolution of internal auditing invariably focus on the westward migration in the United States in the nineteenth century. By the mid-1800s, development in the western half of the country created a need to improve transportation, and it was the burgeoning railroad industry that answered the call. The resulting physical scattering of company assets (rolling stock) and financial transactions (ticket sales along rail routes) decentralized operations. "It was not until the rapid railroad expansion began in the 1840s," according to author James L. Boockholdt, "that companies began to conduct financial transactions at widely dispersed geographic locations. This development required the appointment of internal auditors to monitor the processing of these transactions."[3]

The same economic pressures that created opportunities for the railroad industry and the need for internal auditors also led to the first corporations funded by stockholders. That is a key development in the evolution of modern business and internal auditing. It established a separation not only of management from ownership but the need for the audit function as a check on management.

"As corporations were created, the need developed for reporting to stockholders on the performance of management. The railroads, as the first major enterprises in the United States to rely primarily on outside capital, were also among the first to encounter the need for reporting to the sources of that capital. Examinations by parties independent of management were frequently used to validate management's reports during the nineteenth century."[4]

Those early efforts for independent validation of management reports were taken on by committees of the board, the precursors of today's audit committees. However, the complexity of the task soon required a level of skill and expertise outside the realm of most director-led committees.

"Many of the early audit committees in the United States appear to have been utilized to investigate frauds within their companies. By the middle of the nineteenth century, independent accountants and bookkeepers were in practice in most major cities, and frequently they were engaged to aid audit committees in their investigations."[5]

This outside, or independent, support for validating management reports often included recommendations for improving controls to prevent inaccurate accounts and outright frauds. That planted the seeds for another fundamental of modern auditing — assurance and advice over controls.

The observations from Boockholdt's 1983 article, *Historical Perspective on the Auditor's Role: The Early Experience of the American Railroads*, suggest an early realization of the value of auditing not only on matters of finance but also on internal controls.

The Birth of The IIA

By the mid- to late-1800s, the separation of owners from managers, the dispersal of organizational activity over large areas, and the recognition of the potential for biased reporting from management had firmly established the need for professional auditing. Also established were the concepts of independent and objective assessments and a systematic, disciplined approach to assurance over controls. Having an internal function acting as the eyes and ears of management further cemented the need for internal audit.

However, by the time The IIA was founded, internal auditing was entrenched in providing assurance over the accuracy of financial reporting. From *Internal Auditing: History, Evolution, and Prospects*:

> ". . .internal auditing was still perceived as a closely related extension of the work of external auditors — they were frequently called upon to assist external auditors in financial statement reviews or perform accounting-related functions such as bank reconciliations. Internal auditors were seen to be playing a fairly modest role within organizations and had

only a 'limited responsibility in the total managerial spectrum (Moeller & Witt, 1999).'"[6]

A principal driver to that focus were two landmark Depression-era pieces of U.S. legislation — the Securities Act of 1933 and the Securities Exchange Act of 1934. Those acts, which continue to regulate issuance of securities in primary markets and trading of the securities in secondary markets, include strict requirements on financial reporting.

This is not a criticism of practitioners of that era. Indeed, their assurance work was focused on the greatest needs of their organizations. They were following the risks. Legislation and regulation influencing internal audit's focus is a theme that repeats itself, driving change throughout the profession's history.

But from the 1940s through the 1970s, there was a gradual expansion of internal audit's scope beyond financial assurance. Ramamoorti notes that nearly two decades after the founding of The IIA, the following definition of internal auditing was presented by Brink & Cashin (1958):

> "Internal auditing thus emerges as a special segment of the broad field of accounting, utilizing the basic techniques and method of auditing. The fact that the public accountant and the internal auditor use many of the same techniques often leads to a mistaken assumption that there is little difference in the work or in ultimate objectives. The internal auditor, like any auditor, is concerned with the investigation of the validity of representations, but in his case the representations with which he is concerned cover a much wider range and have to do with many matters, where the relationship to the accounts is often somewhat remote."[7]

It is not surprising that, during this period, The IIA acted as the principal facilitator of internal audit's evolution, primarily by establishing informal standards and responsibilities. For example, the fundamental *Statement of Responsibilities of the Internal Auditor*, first issued in 1947, remained a valuable touchstone for practitioners well into the 1990s.

In 1978, The IIA issued the *Standards for the Professional Practice of Internal Auditing* (*Standards*). That pivotal document helped elevate the profession's stature by clearly communicating its role, scope, and objectives while setting a global standard for practitioners. It also established a benchmark against which internal audit activities are still measured. But equally important, it signaled to stakeholders and the world that internal auditing is a true profession.

At the same time, the importance of having a proper reporting line that helped preserve internal audit's independence from management was becoming increasingly clear. In an early but landmark study on corporate audit committees, Mautz & Neumann (1977) stated:

> "For the most part, the audit committee is viewed as a bridge between the board of directors and the auditors... To fulfill their responsibilities to shareholders and the public at large, audit committee members have had to become more interested in, and better informed on, auditing matters. Management also has become aware of the necessity of protecting itself through adequate attention to internal controls and effective audits. Consequently, it has become more responsive to auditor suggestions and audit committee requests for information."

In similar vein, authors Brink & Witt (1982) noted:

> "In most situations, the internal auditing group has moved to very high levels in all operational areas and has established itself as a valued and respected part of the management effort. To an increasing extent also the internal auditor is serving the board of directors — usually via the audit committee of that board."[8]

The Influences of a Dynamic Risk Landscape

Earlier in this chapter, I noted the influence of legislation and regulation on the scope and focus of internal audit. As risk areas evolve and mature, organizations have consistently steered internal audit to best fit its risk management needs at the time. Clearly, the profession's evolution has been influenced by visceral reactions to scandal.

That was abundantly evident in the first 10 years of the twenty-first century, as major scandals shook the financial world. It began with the Enron and WorldCom debacles, which led to the landmark U.S. Sarbanes-Oxley Act of 2002. That legislation was jokingly referred to as the Internal Auditor Full Employment Act because of the bevy of new regulations that broadly expanded financial reporting compliance risks. As late as 2019, financial reporting compliance still accounted for more than 15% of the typical internal audit plan in the United States.[9] Meanwhile, as the globe was thrust into the Great Recession, banking scandals led to development of the U.S. Dodd-Frank Wall Street Reform and Consumer Protection Act in 2010.

Throughout this century, advances in technology that have disrupted and redefined business models also created a new risk area — the menacing and ubiquitous threat of cyberattacks. But the ultimate disruptive risk may be the emergence of the novel COVID-19 pandemic in early 2020, which opened a Pandora's Box of business continuity, crisis management, and new cyber vulnerabilities.

It is significant that the profession responded by successfully pivoting to the changing demands created by a dynamic risk landscape and new regulations. What's more, The IIA has been instrumental in helping to create tools and frameworks to support evolving risk management.

In 2013 and 2017, respectively, the Committee of Sponsoring Organizations of the Treadway Commission (COSO), of which The IIA is a founding member, released important updates to its signature frameworks on internal controls and enterprise risk management (ERM). Both have become essential amid the growing complexity of governance, risk, and control in a fast-moving world.

Of significance, the updated internal control framework built on the original's focus of designing, implementing, and evaluating the effectiveness of internal control. Meanwhile the ERM framework update helped to clarify just what effective ERM is and is not:

> "Enterprise risk management is not a function or department. It is the culture, capabilities, and practices that organizations integrate with strategy-setting and apply when they carry out that strategy, with the purpose of managing risk in creating, preserving, and realizing value."[10]

The ERM framework's emphasis on "creating, preserving, and realizing value" has also been critical to the evolution of internal audit, as it makes clear that part of the risk management mission is the creation of value.

Beyond their impact on regulations, high-profile corporate scandals this century have fed a growing recognition that culture is often at the core of scandal, and that internal audit has a role to play in assessing culture. Many inside and outside the profession have expressed doubts about internal audit's ability to audit culture effectively, but the profession is making great progress in this area.

One of the most significant contributions to support the evolution of the profession in response to the volatile and dynamic risk landscape was the addition of Core Principles for the Professional Practice of Internal Auditing to the 2017 update to the International Professional Practices Framework (IPPF). But the change is more than just an addition or update to the profession's guidelines. The 10 principles articulate the fundamental beliefs that drive the internal audit profession. Those guideposts are designed to help practitioners remain centered on the core philosophies of internal auditing, even as technology, climate, geopolitics, macroeconomics, and social norms change the world around us.

The IIA's guidance has inexorably moved the profession toward its rightful place as a trusted advisor to management, an equal partner in risk management, and a fundamental component of sound corporate governance. The IIA's 2030 vision statement sets an objective of having the profession "universally recognized as indispensable to effective governance, risk management, and control." By steadily marching forward to a drumbeat of change, we have made palpable progress toward that lofty goal, but achieving it will require further evolution and a mindset that motivates internal auditors to become agents of change.

A Natural Evolution

Looking back at the history of internal auditing, it's clear the profession has never been static. Since its origins nearly 6,000 years ago, our evolution has been extraordinary. As we look forward, we need to consider the next leap in terms of our value proposition. Embracing challenges and opportunities amid the chaos of near constant change is that next leap.

While at times it may seem like for every step we take forward we take two steps back, there is an unmistakable trajectory of progress. New challenges are a call to action to step forward — wherever it may take us. We can never sit on our laurels. Indeed, we are not at all different from other professions. The medical profession has evolved from diagnosing and treating symptoms to developing preventative medicines and encouraging lifestyles that keep people healthier and more resilient and resistant to disease.

So it is with internal auditing. We must provide our organizations with the insight and foresight to not only protect value but help them fulfill their mandate to create value for their investors and stakeholders.

Becoming true agents of change is part of the natural evolution of internal audit.

CHAPTER 2
The Imperative for Change

— • • • • —

Progress is impossible without change, and those who cannot change their minds cannot change anything.

— George Bernard Shaw —

When I assumed my first internal audit role in 1975, the most sophisticated technology in the department was a 10-key calculator, and our data was maintained on 16-column paper pads. We had no fax machine, and desktop and laptop computers were still more than a decade away. Our audit plans were based on a predetermined list of activities and departments that needed to be audited every two to three years. Oh how the internal audit profession has changed! The profession changed because it was imperative that it evolve, and that imperative is likely to drive even more dramatic change in the decade(s) ahead.

As we have seen, there are many factors driving the evolution of internal auditing. For the lion's share of its history, change has happened at a deliberate, methodical pace. The forces of technology and disruption were kept in check by limits on communications, transportation, and science. Part of the challenge of the twenty-first century is that these limits are effectively gone. One example is the latest evolution in mobile connectivity, known as 5G. The impact will be nothing as pedestrian as faster download speeds; it will be in how 5G fuels a "connected everything" world. Connected cars, smart communities, industrial internet of things (IoT), immersive education — these and more will be made possible by 5G.

This transformative technology will increase the volume of data coming into organizations from billions of bytes of data, known as gigabytes, to trillions of gigabytes, known as zettabytes. Indeed, the 50 billion connected devices in the world in 2020 were expected to generate 4.4 zettabytes of data, compared with .1 zettabyte generated in 2013, and that was with only a partial rollout of 5G technology.

It is difficult to grasp the enormity of 5G, but it is easy to predict that organizations will try to leverage the powerful new business tool. That creates a classic risk/opportunity conundrum: Collecting, analyzing, understanding, managing, protecting, and auditing today's data already poses logistical, resource, and talent problems for many organizations. Imagine what it will be like when data streams expand exponentially. Cybersecurity challenges, already a significant concern, are expected to multiply. Complicating the issue is a growing global data privacy movement.

However, the challenge for modern organizations and governments is to not merely survive 5G and other disruptive firestorms but to thrive amid these conflagrations. The reward for those that do is that, just as iron is strengthened by a tempering process, organizations will emerge stronger, more agile, and resilient enough to manage the next firestorm. Just as tempering makes metals less brittle, organizations must learn to manage stress without breaking.

As an integral component to effective risk management and sound governance, internal auditors must become agents of change who support and instigate the tempering process within their organizations. We must expose weaknesses, question conclusions (such as on data), challenge ill-conceived strategies, and promote actions that help create and enhance value. However, to become true agents of change, we must understand and accept the urgency of the moment and realize and take immediate action to overcome our own weaknesses.

Where Internal Audit Is Lagging

The imperative for change in the internal audit profession is rooted in the challenges and complexities wrought by technological disruption and the accelerating velocity of risks. These factors demand assurance and advice that is insightful, prescient, relevant, and trusted. However, in its present state, the profession is not positioned to deliver.

Risk management is difficult. Organizations continually face extraordinary headwinds spawned by a turbulent environment in which risks materialize seemingly overnight. In the second decade of the century, global financial and business markets were rocked by spectacular cybersecurity breaches, corporate failures induced by toxic cultures, and the fallout of sexual assault and harassment in the workplace. The first year of the third decade ushered in a powerful social justice movement, the accelerating effects of climate change, and myriad impacts on economic, cyber, business continuity, and talent-management risks brought on by the global COVID-19 pandemic. While all that may seem extraordinary, it's evident that risk events once thought of as black swans are increasingly becoming routine.

Outdated Processes

Internal auditors must realize and accept that the profession's bread-and-butter processes — annual risk assessments; rigid, risk-based annual audit plans; lengthy audit engagements; verbose, narrative-driven reports — are relics that position practitioners to only address yesterday's challenges. This reinforces my long-held belief that internal audit must take a more continuous approach to risk assessment and assurance — auditing at the speed of risk.

Lisa Lee, chief audit executive (CAE) at Google, laments that even in an organization considered progressive, there can be a tendency for internal audit reports to tell the *how* and not the *why*.

"It never fails: A first draft of any audit report still seems to focus on what we did," Lee said. "Why does that matter? Why should the business care about the work that we did? What matters is the value from insights we bring to them."

In *Exploring the Next Generation of Internal Auditing*, Protiviti EVP of Global Internal Audit Brian Christensen clearly lays out the need for a change in process, especially during a tumultuous period such as the COVID-19 pandemic:

> "The foundation of next-generation internal auditing lies in principles such as agility, real-time risks and controls monitoring, dynamic risk assessments, and the effective leveraging of data and advanced technology. The advantages a next-generation internal audit mindset and approach deliver have become further magnified during this global crisis. Consider risk assessments as just one example. The catastrophic effects of this pandemic are bringing in a whole new look and

examination at the risk assessment process, particularly if this is something typically conducted on an annual or even less-frequent basis. Risk assessments should be structured to respond to risks as quickly as they change. This requires agile methodologies supported by a more in-depth understanding of the risks, as well as the ability to quantitatively measure and monitor those risks. Next-generation internal audit functions have moved beyond annual or quarterly risk updates to obtain a real-time view on changes to risk, their impacts to the organization, and the impact on the assurance needed from internal audit."[1]

Adopting New Technology in Audit Processes

Research also continues to point to a troubling truth about the profession's relationship with technology: It's broken. Despite years of admonitions from The IIA and other leading internal audit voices, the adoption of technology to improve internal audit efficiency remains low. In fact, two recent surveys raised serious concerns about internal audit's commitment to adopting and adapting technology to meet the growing needs of organizations.

Another Protiviti report, *Embracing the Next Generation of Internal Auditing*, based on the firm's Internal Audit Capabilities and Needs survey, found that 3 of 4 internal audit groups were undertaking some form of innovation or transformation. But most were only beginning the journey, and a significant number of functions had yet to even get started. Worse yet, "Less than 1 in 3 internal audit functions currently have a roadmap in place to guide their innovation and transformation journeys."[2]

Foot-dragging on technology is reflected in the profession's continuing struggle to provide assurance to their organizations. Protiviti's report found serious competency gaps within internal audit functions in various IT areas, including cloud computing, auditing IT, mobile applications, big data/business intelligence, IoT, and using/mastering new technology and applications.[3]

Findings from PwC's State of the Internal Audit Profession report, *Elevating Internal Audit's Role: The Digitally Fit Function*, are equally disappointing. PwC defined digital fitness in two important contexts:

- Whether the function has in place the skills and competencies to provide strategic advice to stakeholders and to provide assurance regarding risks from the organization's digital transformation.

- Whether the function is changing its own processes and services to become more data driven and digitally enabled.

In total, 19% of internal audit functions were digitally fit and 27% were taking definitive steps toward digital fitness; however, 54% were described as just starting relevant activities or planning them "in far more ad hoc ways."[4]

That is particularly troubling when one considers how long the profession has been talking about updating and transforming its processes. I addressed many of the same themes in *The Speed of Risk*, where I lamented the profession's low adoption rate of next-generation technology, reliance on weak approaches to identifying emerging and atypical risks, and minimal changes in decades-old auditing processes.

Transformational change was the theme of an IIA Audit Executive Center report, *Pulse of Internal Audit: The Internal Audit Transformation Imperative*, which urged practitioners to embrace agility, innovate, raise the level of talent, and engage more closely with boards. The closing words of the report are as relevant and urgent as ever:

> "Internal audit's progress over the past, and the successes accomplished, will not be enough to carry the profession forward. Current times require changes in mindset and actions from all internal auditors. Complacency will lead to irrelevance, but decisive moves by CAEs will propel internal audit forward through the transformation required."

As risks grow more complex with every new technological disruption, stakeholders are demanding more from internal audit. Reports such as the ones from The IIA, Protiviti, and PwC suggest the profession may not be ready to meet those demands.

We must ask ourselves two key questions:

- Why is where we are today not good enough?
- What can we do about it?

Our Trusted Processes Can't Keep Up with the Speed of Risk

Internal audit must make a concerted and coordinated effort to modernize its processes and approach to assurance and advisory services. COVID-19 increased awareness of the need for more frequent updates, not just to audit plans but also to risk assessments. Indeed, 6 in 10 internal auditors globally said their functions updated audit plans, identified emerging risks, and reviewed risk assessments in the wake of the fast-spreading coronavirus, according to three IIA surveys conducted in the first months after a pandemic was declared.

Part of any revolution must include a change in how we adapt and adopt technology. For example, the profession is slow to embrace the use of robotics process automation (RPA) and artificial intelligence (AI). Those will be vital tools if we hope to not just manage but understand and leverage the tidal wave of data that will soon be available because of 5G and other still-unseen technological advances.

The Internal Audit Mindset Is to Pivot to Change, Not Anticipate or Initiate It

I have written and spoken about the value of foresight from internal auditors. But, historically, the profession's greatest changes have been in *response* to evolving stakeholder needs.

Internal auditors have cultivated a long and respected legacy as purveyors of hindsight. Almost all of us are adept at looking at the past year's data and telling management where mistakes were made. But such hindsight has become one of our least valuable skills. Often, our clients are fully aware of past mistakes and likely are looking only for solutions or recommendations for the future.

Meanwhile, with the advent of operational auditing and, ultimately, the introduction of consulting/advice into our portfolio of services, we also became purveyors of insight. Although more valuable than hindsight, it also suffers from limitations in an era when risks are emerging at warp speed. Today's insight may well be tomorrow's hindsight.

There will always be a need for both hindsight and insight. But in an era of near constant change, stakeholders seek to navigate the future more than revisit the past or dwell in the present. That's why we need to concentrate on the risks of tomorrow and provide foresight if we are to not only protect but enhance and create value for our organizations. As purveyors of foresight, our roles as agents of change will enable us to make a difference in the organizations we serve.

The Internal Audit Mindset Focuses on Protecting Value, Not Creating It

Let's begin our look at this issue by examining The IIA's Three Lines Model, published in mid-2020. An update to the widely accepted Three Lines of Defense Model, the Three Lines Model is built on the premise that risk management and sound governance cannot fixate on only defending or protecting value. In my view, this is the chief improvement over the original model.

The introduction to the new Three Lines Model report focuses on four key points that optimize the model for use by any organization:

- Adopting a principles-based approach and adapting the model to suit organizational objectives and circumstances.
- Focusing on the contribution risk management makes to achieving objectives and creating value, as well as to matters of "defense" and protecting value.
- Clearly understanding the roles and responsibilities represented in the model and the relationships among them.
- Implementing measures to ensure activities and objectives are aligned with the prioritized interests of stakeholders.

Additionally, the new model lays out six key principles that help define good governance, the roles of key players in the governance process, the importance and value of independent assurance, and the concept of creating, not just protecting, value. Principle 6 focuses squarely on creating and protecting value:

> All roles working together collectively contribute to the creation and protection of value when they are aligned with each other and with the prioritized interests of stakeholders. Alignment of activities is achieved through communication, cooperation, and collaboration. This ensures the reliability, coherence, and transparency of information needed for risk-based decision-making.

The concept of defining internal audit's value to the organization simply as helping to protect value is outdated. Our stakeholders demand more, and internal auditors must rid themselves of this mindset.

We Are Resistant to Change

Change is hard. It is fraught with uncertainty. It questions our abilities. It disrupts what we see as an already challenging and complex job. It also is true that, without change, any profession will plateau, eventually decline, and become irrelevant.

Rosabeth Moss Kanter, an Arbuckle Professor at Harvard Business School and director and chair of the Harvard University Advanced Leadership Initiative, offers *10 Reasons Why People Resist Change*:[5]

1. **Loss of control.** Our sense of self-determination is often the first thing to go when faced with a potential change coming from someone else.
2. **Excess uncertainty.** People will often prefer to remain mired in misery than to head toward an unknown. As the saying goes, "Better the devil you know than the devil you don't know."
3. **Surprise, surprise!** Sudden change is often resisted. It's always easier to say "no" than to say "yes."
4. **Everything seems different.** People are creatures of habit. Routines become automatic, but change jolts us into consciousness, sometimes in uncomfortable ways.
5. **Loss of face.** When change involves a big shift of strategic direction, the people responsible for the previous direction dread the perception that they must have been wrong.
6. **Concerns about competence.** Change is resisted when it makes people feel stupid. They might express skepticism, but down deep they are worried that their skills will be obsolete.
7. **More work.** Change is indeed more work.
8. **Ripple effects.** Pushback is inevitable. Ripples of change disrupt other departments, important customers, and people well outside the venture.
9. **Past resentments.** The ghosts of the past remain out of sight if everything is in a steady state. But trying something new can reopen old wounds and bring out historic resentments.
10. **Sometimes the threat is real.** Change is resisted because it can hurt. When new technologies displace old ones, jobs can be lost.

While it is important to understand why we resist change, it is not an excuse. The case for change in internal audit is clear and compelling.

Sometimes, Management Is Happy to Keep Us in Our Safe Place

This may be the most insidious enabler of the profession's resistance to change. Despite being allies, management and internal audit do not always see eye to eye. Disagreements may be easily resolved by a simple rewording in an audit report, or they may be serious enough to impair internal audit's ability to carry out its mission.

This natural tension also can lead to management taking advantage of internal audit's inertia. I have witnessed many cases over my 45 years in the profession where a strong internal audit function is not welcomed by corporate and government executives who would rather keep it as window dressing and not as a window to corporate or government accountability. In 2015, I wrote about this scenario in the context of underpaying the CAE, but it also can apply to allowing internal audit to become entrenched in its comfort zone.

What Can We Do About It?

It is important to step back and look at how the imperative for change fits into the bigger picture for the profession and for overall governance within our organizations. As part of its strategic plan, The IIA's 2030 vision statement set a lofty goal: *Internal audit professionals are universally recognized as indispensable to effective governance, risk management, and control.*[6] I believe that being value creators, not just value protectors, is integral to being universally recognized as indispensable. But bluntly, we've got a long way to go.

The answer to "What can we do about it?" is clear. As a profession, internal audit must aggressively seek ways to update processes that can keep pace with the speed of risk and abandon those that cannot. We must truly embrace technology once and for all. We must alter our mindset to focus on creating value, not just protecting it. And we must recognize our shortcomings and commit to improving them.

Plainly, it is much easier to articulate what must be done than to go out and achieve it. However, as we embark on achieving indispensability, we need to ensure our zeal for change doesn't overtake our common sense. I believe there are five things we must get right as we move forward:

1. **Be a beacon for emerging risks.** This means being a steady and reliable resource of information, assurance, and clear-eyed advice to management and the board on data ethics, AI governance, and sustainability. Those three issues will have oversized influence on risk and risk management in the coming decade.

2. **Recruit, retrain, and retain game-changing talent.** It is vital that we have the right people to update our processes and help shape our new mindset as agents of change. We must be open to having such talent come from outside internal audit and finance. As late as 2018, about three-quarters of CAEs polled for The IIA's *Pulse of Internal Audit* report found accounting, finance, or IT-related degrees most desirable. Business, operational, technical, and communications backgrounds lagged well behind.[7] The same survey found that half of CAEs described skills such as data mining/analytics and cybersecurity as only somewhat or not essential skills.

The dire need for both skillsets could not be clearer today. As demand grows for these talents, it will become increasingly difficult to hire the people we need to transform our processes. CAEs will need to focus on building desired skills within existing staff. Whether hiring from within or outside the organization, building a strategic plan to ensure a steady supply of qualified personnel is critical.

3. **Be champions for strong governance.** By example and through audit work, internal auditors should support sound governance. Principles of sound governance can be found in both COSO frameworks, the new Three Lines Model, and The IIA's American Corporate Governance Index's Guiding Principles of Corporate Governance. By helping to ensure our organizations have effective and efficient governance, internal audit adds value and positions itself to effect necessary change.

4. **Innovate for greater efficiency and impact.** We have seen admirable advances in adapting agile work processes pioneered in software development to audit engagement processes. Rather than the traditional linear steps involving planning, fieldwork, review, and reporting, agile internal auditing uses sprints, where those four components are performed simultaneously in a cycle of one to two weeks. The sprints are repeated until the audit is completed.

Improved collaboration, better transparency, and faster turnaround are the clear benefits cited by proponents such as Jamie DuBray, western hemisphere audit manager for oilfield services company Schlumberger. DuBray reports the company adopted agile auditing techniques in 2019 and saw average target deliveries for audits cut from 45 days to five days.

This kind of innovation is what will transform internal auditing. From DuBray's perspective, the profession has two options — innovate or become irrelevant. "I don't think we want to be labeled in a way that we are not being relevant. We'll die as a profession if we don't keep up," she said.[8]

5. **Be prolific in telling internal audit's story — how we preserve and CREATE value.** Internal auditors are too often self-effacing and reticent to speak out when it comes to creating awareness about the value we bring to our organizations. This can be partially blamed on the misguided idea that projecting and protecting our reputation for objectivity requires being modest. We can remain objective and independent and still speak boldly about the profession's rightful place as a vital player in risk management and sound governance.

I examine how to achieve these goals in part two, "Enacting the Change," looking specifically at changing our mindset, revolutionizing our processes, leveraging technology, and telling our story.

Next Steps

I debated whether to use a crossroads analogy to hammer home the key message of this chapter. At first, I thought it a bit cliché. Every crisis doesn't have to be a choice of one path or another. But in this case, a slight modification to the crossroads concept offers an important level of clarity and urgency to illustrate the need for change.

Most people envision a crossroads as intersecting roads that offer alternatives on which way to go. But that vision is two-dimensional, like the x- and y-axes on a quadrant graph. The reality is that there is a third dimension.

In this case, the z-axis offers a measure of how steep the journey toward change has become. Until we commit as a profession to innovate our approaches, update stale and slow processes, and embrace technology, the grade will get steeper with each passing day. The other direction on the z-axis provides an easier road. Of course, that road is all downhill, which is a direction we can't afford to go.

I've addressed questions of why where we are today is not good enough and what we can do about it. This leads to a third question: Who will lead us through this change? The answer should be obvious by now — the agents of change among us.

CHAPTER 3
Independence Doesn't Imply Isolation

— • • • • —

It's not about standing still and becoming safe. If anybody wants to keep creating, they have to be about change.

— Miles Davis —

The imperative for a new and critical step in the evolution of internal audit is evident. The pace of change in technology and disruption demands next-level internal audit services enabled by a specific mindset and skillset. We have discussed the need for internal auditors to be agents of change, but what exactly does that mean?

In the simplest terms, agents of change are individuals or internal audit functions that are catalysts for transformation that creates value within their organizations. We will get into the details of just what that entails, but for the moment let's first address how today's internal auditors typically approach their jobs. Most internal auditors are conditioned from their first day on the job to pursue a "systematic and disciplined" approach when undertaking internal audit engagements rooted in independence and objectivity. While those are all essential elements of the formal definition of internal auditing, they must be practiced with the overarching objective of adding value and improving an organization's operations, which are also essential elements of the definition.

Today's internal auditors have, for the most part, evolved to a point where they are comfortable providing both assurance and advisory services. I recently articulated what I call the "Five A's of Effective Internal Auditing" to convey what internal auditors should strive to accomplish:

Assess risks. Successfully assessing the organization's risks is fundamental to the job of internal auditing. Internal auditors first and foremost must follow the risks. However, we must aim for a broad perspective on how we assess those risks. Beyond identifying those things that threaten to disrupt or impede the organization from achieving its goals, we should assess the adequacy of risk management, organizational governance, and culture. We should understand the board's appetite for risk and evaluate whether executive management is operating within those bounds. To do those things, we must have a keen understanding of the organization's goals and strategies, as well as the industry in which the organization operates.

Align internal audit coverage to focus on the most critical risks. The surest path to failure for internal auditors is paved with personal preferences and priorities. The reason we assess risks is to clearly identify the areas where we need to focus. Fixating on risks with a lower likelihood of materializing, or those whose impact on the organization are likely to be insignificant, will diminish the perceived value of internal audit and ultimately lead to irrelevance. However, internal auditors should never make the mistake of thinking that they must be in lockstep with management in assessing risks or aligning coverage. Having a thorough understanding of goals and strategies, and consistently aligning internal audit with them, offers practitioners the opportunity to provide additional insight and foresight.

Assure management and the board that risks are effectively managed and controls are effectively designed and implemented. This is the legacy service of internal audit. It is essential to protecting value within an organization. Assurance over the effectiveness of financial reporting, compliance, operations, cybersecurity, and other areas affords comfort to management and the board that risks within the organization are effectively managed. Before we can offer such assurance, however, we must have carefully planned, conducted, and reported the results of our engagements. If we identify problems, we should be able to articulate the condition, effect, cause, criteria, and recommendations. Of particular importance is making sure we dig deep enough to expose the root causes of risk management or control failures and weaknesses.

Additionally, assurance over organizational governance and culture takes on more subjective measurements and mandates greater practitioner judgment. Some internal auditors are less comfortable auditing the "soft stuff," but this is increasingly vital to providing effective overall assurance.

Advise management and the board by drawing on our vast expertise. As the risk landscape becomes increasingly complex and fast-paced for most organizations — fed by technology and its disruptive influences — internal audit's advisory services are more important than ever. After all, there is little value in informing stakeholders that mistakes were made when we could have helped to avert the mistakes by advising during design and execution. Assurance is an accurate look in the rearview mirror. However, as every driver knows, accidents are avoided by being aware of your surroundings and — most importantly — looking ahead.

Anticipate tomorrow's risks. The ability to anticipate the organization's needs, as well as its risks, raises internal audit's profile and value. Having a grasp on emerging risks, disruptive technologies, and threats that lie just beyond the horizon helps to make internal audit indispensable. If we are unable to anticipate risks, it is unlikely that we will be able to effectively audit at the speed of risk.

When executed well, the impressive list of services internal audit offers can provide significant value to any organization. But we should take a moment to dive a bit deeper into what internal audit must do to add value and remain relevant.

As noted in the section above on aligning internal audit coverage, "Fixating on risks with a lower likelihood of materializing or risks whose impact on the organization are likely to be insignificant will diminish the perceived value of internal audit, and ultimately lead to irrelevance." In his book, *Ready and Relevant: Prepare to Audit What Matters Most*, author Tim Berichon puts into prescient perspective related statistics on relevance from a recent IIA *Pulse of Internal Audit* report.

> "The Pulse reported that only 45% of chief audit executives (CAEs) feel that their internal audit departments are very agile, yet 67% already realize that agility is extremely important in the future. It was surprising that this percentage was not higher, and also surprising that these CAEs feel it is important 'in the future' and not more urgently now. . .

In response to disruption, the Pulse reported that only 56% of respondents have meaningful collaboration with other lines of defense, 46% have flexible resource planning and allocation, and 36% have flexible talent management. Yet these areas are all very important to help internal audit be more responsive to strategically important matters.

The Pulse also noted that 62% perform work only to the extent of internal capabilities and 65% delay work until they have developed the competencies/skills, or they exclude the area altogether. But what if the topic is very important to the enterprise? It's no wonder internal auditors sometimes feel they are not responsive enough and wonder why they are not more relevant."[1]

Berichon goes on to quote Sir Richard Branson, the English business magnate, investor, author, philanthropist, and founder of Virgin Group, who said, "If someone offers you an amazing opportunity and you're not sure you can do it, say yes — then learn how to do it later."[2]

The bottom line on relevance is that you may perform stellar internal audits that expose control weaknesses or failures and identify root causes, but if they do not focus on areas of importance to the organization, they are not likely to add value. I have always referred to them as the "so what" audits, because management and the board may well say in response to the audit report, "All of that may be true, but it is also not important."

Internal auditors should assess risks, align internal audit coverage to focus on imminent risks, assure management and the board that risks are effectively managed and controls are effectively designed and implemented, advise management and the board by drawing on our vast expertise, and anticipate tomorrow's risk. All that should be accomplished while remaining focused on the organization's goals and strategies. Any practitioner reading the list might say, "Whew, isn't that enough?" In a word, "no."

The challenges today's organizations face are complex, volatile, and often overwhelming. Contributing to overall success requires those in critical roles, such as internal audit, to help the organization in every way possible. For internal audit, that means doing more than providing value. We must also contribute to value creation. We must do more than check to see if all the doors are locked. We must also help the organization decide where new doors should be. If we walk away and things are no better than when we came, we haven't been successful. If our intent is to fix things, and that's all we care about, we are not agents of change — we are agents of correction. We must take the extra step, go the extra mile, and strive to make it *better* than it was before.

It is important to realize that being an agent of change is not a line of service. It is an outcome that is inspired by how we approach our mission. Agents of change are trusted advisors who offer insight and foresight designed not just to fix things that are broken but transform things so they are better. Value that accrues makes the organization more successful.

Independence and Objectivity

Let's next examine how internal audit came to take on the role of an independent and objective assessor of management activities, what that means in a modern organizational context, and how that relates to agents of change.

As discussed in chapter 1, the concept of independent reporting on management activities began with the creation and growth of corporations in the nineteenth century, when non-management parties were first used to validate management's reports to corporate boards and shareholders. Over time, the task of verifying management reports fell to internal auditors, which is a key evolution from simply being management's monitors of transaction processes.

In his article on internal audit history, Sridhar Ramamoorti notes that internal audit started out protecting against payroll fraud and other asset losses, expanded its role to verification of all financial transactions, and "gradually moved from an 'audit for management' emphasis to an 'audit of management' approach (Reeve, 1986)."[3]

He provides additional context in a related endnote, where he addresses the oft-quoted issue of "serving two masters." In brief, there is a predictable conflict between internal audit working for the betterment of the overall organization, which requires the support and cooperation of management, and the unavoidable critique of management performance that comes from internal audit carrying out its duties. Naturally, tensions can rise when internal auditors are expected to carry out their work "fearlessly recognizing their ultimate allegiance to those charged with organizational governance, not management."[4]

This conflict of working operationally for management while serving the interests of the organization overall is addressed in the *International Standards for the*

Professional Practice of Internal Auditing (Standards). Standard 1100 – Independence and Objectivity states, "The internal audit activity must be independent, and internal auditors must be objective in performing their work."

The related interpretation from the *Standards* then identifies a key concept of the "dual-reporting relationship," which has internal audit reporting administratively to management and functionally to the board. "To achieve the degree of independence necessary to effectively carry out the responsibilities of the internal audit activity, the chief audit executive has direct and unrestricted access to senior management and the board. This can be achieved through a dual-reporting relationship."[5]

The conclusion is that independence provides internal audit the confidence and ability to review and potentially be critical of the work of management without fear of reprisal.

We have yet to address the role of objectivity in internal audit and how it relates to internal audit independence. It is important not to conflate the two concepts. Indeed, doing so can act as a barrier to serving as agents of change.

Practitioners are quick to embrace and protect internal audit's independence from management, but they must realize as employees of the organization they are not independent of the organizations they serve. Employee or contractor, internal auditors depend on the organization that pays them. Dependence, however, does not preclude objectivity.

Objectivity is an unbiased mental attitude that allows internal auditors to go into an engagement with no preconceived notion of what they are going to find and perform their work without compromise. Standard 1120 – Individual Objectivity covers this well by stating, "Internal auditors must have an impartial, unbiased attitude and avoid any conflict of interest."[6]

Objectivity is critically important in that it promotes internal audit as a true broker of assurance. When internal audit reports on the health or weakness of a control or process, its objectivity is at the heart of its credibility.

As the role of internal audit evolved and it was asked to do more for the organization, the likelihood of conflicts that could weaken that independence and objectivity increased. Standard 1130 – Impairment to Independence or Objectivity requires any impairment of independence or objectivity, in fact or in appearance, to be disclosed. Moreover, its related subsections address how and by whom assurance and consulting services may be provided under various scenarios.[7]

That includes the steps to take when conflicts invariably occur. For example, as the use of ERM has gained widespread acceptance, many organizations have assigned the work of overseeing such programs to CAEs. This creates at least a perceived impairment regarding the provision of assurance over the ERM function. Standard 1130.A2 addresses this: "Assurance engagements for functions over which the chief audit executive has responsibility must be overseen by a party outside the internal audit activity."[8]

Maintaining Independence and Objectivity as an Agent of Change

This examination of independence and objectivity brings us to a point where we now can address whether acting as agents of change — and embracing the mindset of helping the organization create value — is a threat to internal audit independence or objectivity.

Acting for the betterment of the overall organization by assisting or supplementing management's efforts to achieve goals and objectives should never be viewed as a compromise of independence or objectivity. Management is not the adversary. The *Standards* set out clear directions on how and when CAEs should disclose real or perceived conflicts and how to manage those conflicts when they invariably occur. Internal audit's obligation to the organization's success should be paramount in this discussion. However, that is not always the case.

Too often, protecting internal audit's independence and objectivity is used as a crutch or an excuse to avoid taking on new roles or speaking out, even when doing so would better serve the organization. This is particularly true when it comes to advisory services. Some practitioners avoid giving advice under the guise of avoiding conflicts to independence and objectivity.

However, objectivity doesn't come on the front end of advice. It comes on the back end. The earliest point at which objectivity could be impaired is when internal audit must go back and audit something on which it provided advice. Additionally, there are the safeguards I mentioned that can be built into advisory activities to avoid such conflicts.

One of my earliest experiences in an advisory role came when I served as the U.S. Army's director of internal review (audit) at the Pentagon. The U.S. Department of Defense was undertaking a massive project to reengineer travel-expense reimbursement for its more than two million military members and civilian employees around the world. I was asked by the assistant secretary of the Army to serve on a taskforce advising the team designing the new travel reimbursement system. Traditionally, it would have been unheard of for an internal auditor to be in the room when controls were being designed. After all, how could we audit them later? But staying out of the room would mean that the team would be lacking a valuable perspective on control design and implementation. I came away from the experience with a much better appreciation for the value we can add on the front end of important initiatives. Although my role was not critical to the success of the project, I was proud that I had served as an agent of change.

The Three Lines Model

It may be beneficial to look at thought leadership on governance and risk management and the role internal audit plays within the overall organization. The new Three Lines Model provides an overdue update to the trusted risk management tool, and it addresses a key criticism of the old Three Lines of Defense Model that it was focused on protecting and not creating value.

One significant change was the greater incorporation of the governing body into the model. The Three Lines Model clearly delineates roles and responsibilities of the governing body, as well as executive management and internal audit. Those roles are not limited to risk management, but they also focus on overall governance of the organization.

While not a governance model, the increased focus on governance supports both value creation and protection and deals with both the offensive and defensive aspects of managing risk.

The Three Line Model is built around six key principles:

- **Principle 1:** Governance of an organization requires appropriate structures and processes that enable accountability, action, and assurance.
- **Principle 2:** Governing body roles ensure appropriate structures and processes are in place for effective governance.

- **Principle 3:** Management's responsibility to achieve organizational objectives comprises both first- and second-line roles. First-line roles are most directly aligned with the delivery of products and/or services to clients of the organization and include the roles of support functions. Second-line roles provide assistance with managing risk.

- **Principle 4:** In its third-line role, internal audit provides independent and objective assurance and advice on the adequacy and effectiveness of governance and risk management. It achieves this through the competent application of systematic and disciplined processes, expertise, and insight. It may consider assurance from other internal and external providers.

- **Principle 5:** Internal audit's independence from the responsibilities of management is critical to its objectivity, authority, and credibility.

- **Principle 6:** All roles working collectively contribute to the creation and protection of value when they are aligned with each other and with the prioritized interests of stakeholders.

Most internal auditors should be familiar with these concepts, even if they hadn't before been articulated in a single model or document. Organizations that embrace and embed them in their controls, operations, and cultures will invariably enjoy stronger governance. Adherence should be the goal of all organizations and, once achieved, the concepts should be continually monitored and nurtured.

The new model's principles-based approach was designed to provide users greater flexibility. Governing bodies, executive management, and internal audit are not slotted into rigid lines or roles. The "lines" concept was retained in the interest of familiarity. However, they are not intended to denote structural elements but a useful differentiation in roles. The areas of responsibility are generally:

- Accountability by the governing body to stakeholders for oversight.
- Actions (including managing risk) by management to achieve organizational objectives.
- Assurance and advice by an independent internal audit function to provide insight, confidence, and encouragement for continuous improvement.

Some have argued that internal audit should remain well within the "third line" out of an abundance of caution to ensure the independence and objectivity of its staff. However, the refreshed model clearly emphasizes that "independence does not imply isolation." As the update notes, "There must be regular interaction between internal audit and management. . . . There is a need for collaboration and communication across both the first- and second-line roles of management and internal audit."

The point bears repeating: Independence does not imply isolation. This is critical to understanding how internal audit can and should act to create value.

We've addressed how modern internal audit is still evolving into a function that creates value for organizations and how perceived threats to independence and objectivity can hinder providing next-level service. We've also addressed how the new Three Lines Model can help dispel a misguided ivory tower mentality about internal audit's independence and objectivity and its role in the organization.

Now for some good news.

How We See Ourselves

To prepare for this book, a global poll of CAEs was conducted by The IIA's Audit Executive Center. The survey disclosed that 9 in 10 respondents believe it is appropriate for internal audit functions to act as agents of change. That should be a cause for celebration. A vast majority of CAEs embrace this new mindset that is critical to the profession's continued evolution. However, data from the same survey reflect that the support has not yet translated into meaningful action.

Only 2 in 10 respondents view themselves as agents of change who partner with executive management to drive change that creates value (see **exhibit 3-1**). Nearly as many (15%) say they facilitate change, but it is up to management to drive change. However, nearly half say they use assurance and consulting services to add value and advocate for change. That is encouraging, as this option comes closest to creating value without actually being agents of change.

It is also important to see how others within the organization view internal audit's role as agents of change, as judged from the responding CAEs' perspective. The survey found that 37% of respondents believe management is fully supportive of internal audit driving change within the organization, and 46% said their boards are fully supportive. That may not be resounding support from our stakeholders, but it's a start. We should take this as a challenge to educate our stakeholders about the potential internal audit holds for creating value.

Exhibit 3-1: 2 in 10 CAEs Operate as Agents of Change

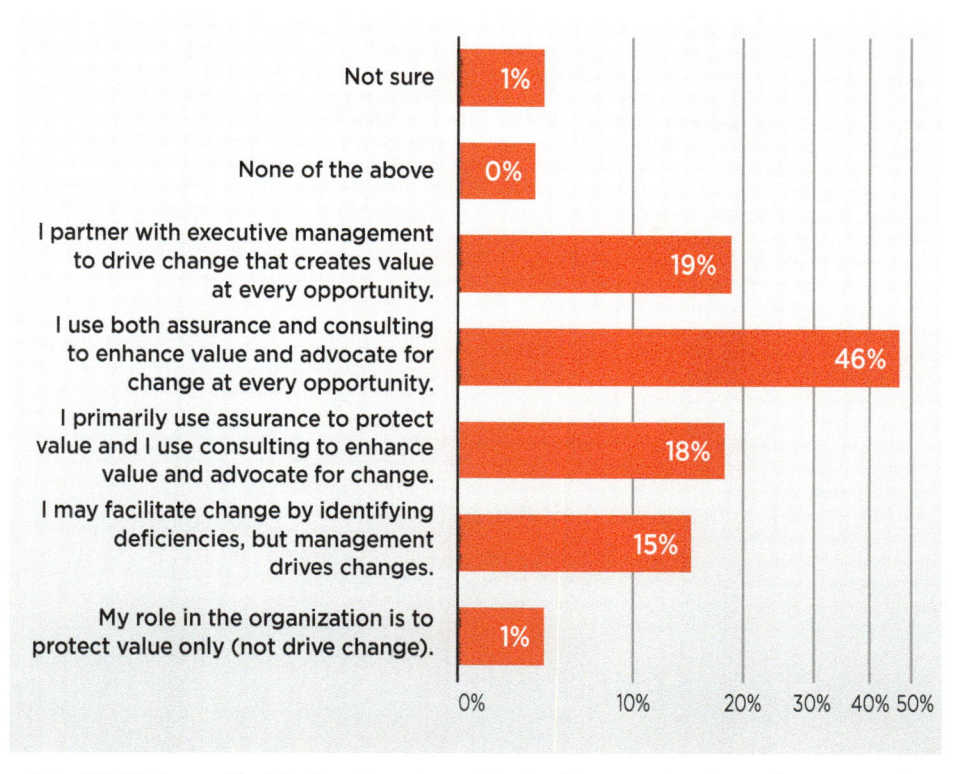

Response	Percentage
Not sure	1%
None of the above	0%
I partner with executive management to drive change that creates value at every opportunity.	19%
I use both assurance and consulting to enhance value and advocate for change at every opportunity.	46%
I primarily use assurance to protect value and I use consulting to enhance value and advocate for change.	18%
I may facilitate change by identifying deficiencies, but management drives changes.	15%
My role in the organization is to protect value only (not drive change).	1%

Note: Q12: Which one of the following statements most closely reflects your view of yourself as an Agent of Change in your organization? n = 586

We should take heart that half of the CAEs said their internal audit function is viewed as an agent of change within the organization (see **exhibit 3-2**). While not yet an overwhelming mandate, this clearly suggests a strong movement toward an evolution of internal audit as an agent of change.

Key Characteristics of Change Agents

Audit leaders expressed clear views on the attributes they believe are required to be agents of change. Their top choices reflect a strong focus on business skills and knowing and understanding their organizations. About 6 in 10 respondents listed business acumen, understanding organizational objectives, and building relationships as key attributes (see **exhibit 3-3**).

Exhibit 3-2: Half of Internal Audit Functions Viewed as Change Agents

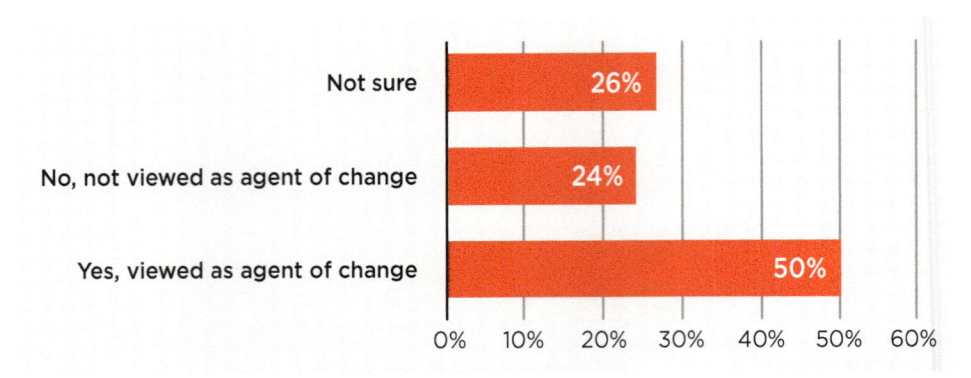

Response	Percentage
Not sure	26%
No, not viewed as agent of change	24%
Yes, viewed as agent of change	50%

Note: Q9: Is the internal audit function within your organization viewed as an Agent of Change? n = 606

Exhibit 3-3: Key Attributes of Change Agents

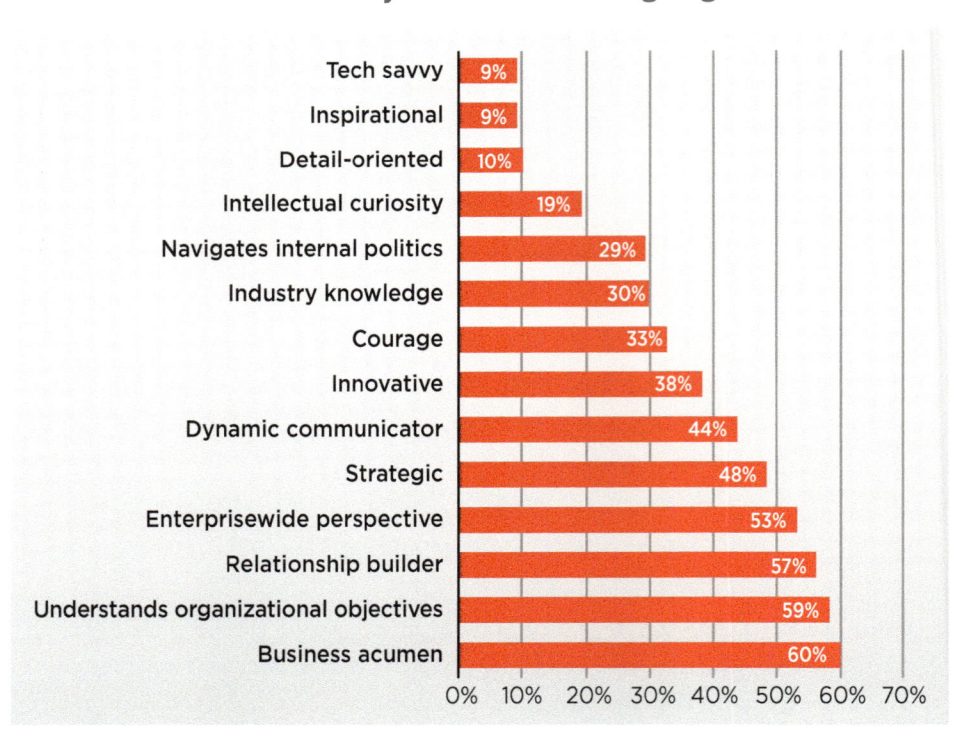

Attribute	Percentage
Tech savvy	9%
Inspirational	9%
Detail-oriented	10%
Intellectual curiosity	19%
Navigates internal politics	29%
Industry knowledge	30%
Courage	33%
Innovative	38%
Dynamic communicator	44%
Strategic	48%
Enterprisewide perspective	53%
Relationship builder	57%
Understands organizational objectives	59%
Business acumen	60%

Note: Q10: What are the most important attributes an internal auditor must demonstrate to be a successful Agent of Change? n = 606

The question is similar to one used to collect data for *Trusted Advisors: Key Attributes of Outstanding Internal Auditors*. The key attributes from the trusted advisors survey were grouped into three broad categories — professional, personal, and relational. The same treatment for data from the agents of change survey sheds additional light on how change agents are viewed by audit leaders. **Exhibit 3-4** categorizes each attribute and adds their ranking from the survey in parenthesis.

Exhibit 3-4: Categories and Rankings of Key Attributes

Professional	Personal	Relational
Business acumen (1)	Innovative (7)	Relationship builder (3)
Understands organizational objectives (2)	Courage (8)	Navigates internal politics (10)
Enterprisewide perspective (4)	Intellectual curiosity (11)	Dynamic communicator (6)
Strategic (5)	Detail-oriented (12)	
Industry knowledge (9)	Inspirational (13)	
Tech savvy (14)		

Four of the top five attributes fall into the professional category, suggesting that respondents see building professional skills as critical to becoming agents of change. Building relationships and being a dynamic communicator from the relational attributes come next. More innate personal attributes, such as being courageous, innovative, and intellectually curious, fall into the bottom half.

We'll examine in more detail how all these attributes translate into individual actions in part three of this book, but it may be valuable to hear now from those who have "walked the talk" as change agents.

Hearing from the Change Agents

Interestingly, the attributes identified in the bottom half of the survey do not align with the views of CAEs who are considered change agent pioneers. These individuals were more likely to list courage and innovation as their top attributes.

Theresa Grafenstine, the former longtime inspector general for the U.S. House of Representatives and current global chief auditor, technology at Citi, identifies courage as her top attribute. "A lot of people associate courage with job functions that put people in potential physical harm, like a police officer or a member of the military, and those obviously require courage," she said. "But as an auditor, having and standing by your convictions, even when it's scary, takes courage."

Courage also is required to challenge conventional thought, and it is critical to sending a clear message to others within the internal audit function about its value, she said. "I would say to CAEs not only is it important for you to go in with that courage and to be able to stand toe to toe, but you need to do that also for your staff. Oftentimes, you're bringing them to these very high-stakes meetings. If they see you kind of buckle . . ."

Brian Foster, former Microsoft general manager over internal audit and current head of internal audit at ServiceNow, sees intellectual curiosity, understanding the details of the business, and being a dynamic communicator as three essential skills for change agents. Two of the three — intellectual curiosity and detail-oriented — ranked near the bottom of the CAE survey.

"The first thing I look for is people who don't just accept the status quo," Foster said. "You know, they love to ask 'why?' It's like the five-year-old who asks why 74 times in a row. But truly, let's challenge why things are done the way they are."

This attribute reflects a curiosity to understand and challenge how things are done. That requires being comfortable in the details, Foster said, but then being able to communicate clearly and concisely to those at the executive level to make a case for change.

For Naohiro Mouri, executive vice president and chief auditor at American International Group Inc., it is a combination of skills that includes subject matter expertise and strong communications. But, he said, it begins with an ability to think differently, which falls into the categories of thinking innovatively and being intellectually curious. Both of those attributes are in the bottom half of the survey results. "I look for the ability to think differently from what we've been doing, being open, being flexible," Mouri said.

Personal Attributes: Nurture or Nature?

The book *Trusted Advisors* describes personal attributes as focusing on "who internal auditors are at the very core of their being. These attributes are ingrained in outstanding internal auditors." But does that preclude that attributes such as being innovative, courageous, intellectually curious, detail-oriented, and inspirational cannot be learned?

Those personal attributes are deeply seated within the best internal auditors, but that doesn't mean each was born with an instinct to innovate, question norms, or battle dragons. Indeed, those are learned attributes nurtured over a lifetime, and each can grow or wane over time.

For example, courage is often discussed as a necessary trait for internal auditors, and over the decades, countless practitioners have put their livelihoods on the line to bring wrongdoing to light. Like many others, I have long believed that Cynthia Cooper, the former vice president of internal audit at WorldCom, is the model of courage in our profession. Her story is well known within internal audit and accounting circles, and she is rightly praised and lauded for having the courage to stand up in the face of enormous pressure and adversity to unearth the $3.8 billion fraud.

In her book, *Extraordinary Circumstances: The Journey of a Corporate Whistleblower*, Cooper counsels internal auditors to "find your courage." But courage doesn't suddenly blossom within an internal auditor simply because there is an expectation or a strong case for it. Cooper's admonition requires practitioners to examine what courage is and under what circumstances their own internal fortitude may be tested.

Courage means more than just speaking out to address a wrongdoing. It also takes courage to admit one's mistakes or step out of our comfort zone. Indeed, stepping out of our comfort zone is critical to becoming an agent of change. The benefits to our internal audit functions, our organizations, and ourselves greatly outweigh the risks.

As internal auditors, we should follow the advice of American businessman Edward Whitacre Jr., who said, "Be willing to step outside your comfort zone once in a while; take the risks in life that seem worth taking. The ride might not be as predictable if you'd just planted your feet and stayed put, but it will be a heck of a lot more interesting."[9]

Trusted Advisors versus Agents of Change

By now you may be asking yourself: What is the difference between a "trusted advisor" and an "agent of change?" The answer may not be evident by merely comparing the definitions I have formulated for the two terms:

> **Trusted advisor:** An internal auditor who builds and sustains trust throughout the organization by leveraging personal, relational, and professional skills and expertise. Trusted advisors are a valued resource in helping organizations enhance risk management and internal controls through assurance and advice.

> **Agents of change:** Internal auditors or internal audit functions that are catalysts for transformation that *create* value within their organizations.

Simply put, I believe that all agents of change must be trusted advisors, but not all trusted advisors are agents of change. A CEO and others in management should constantly be attuned to the perspectives of trusted advisors. These men and women should have a seat at the table and bring an array of skills and expertise that will help the CEO and others make decisions that benefit the organization. By contrast, agents of change will not only have a seat at the table, they will always be armed with transformational ideas. Agents of change won't rest until they have not only offered advice but also had a transformative impact on the organization.

PART TWO

ENACTING THE CHANGE

CHAPTER 4
Agent Change Thyself

— • • • • —

Growth is painful. Change is painful. But nothing is as painful as staying stuck somewhere you don't belong.

— N.R. Narayana Murthy —

We have all heard the expression, "Physician heal thyself." It is an ancient proverb that counsels us to attend to our own defects before those in others.[1] In this chapter, we examine how internal audit practitioners should undertake to improve their own work and the operations of their functions as part of their journeys to becoming agents of change.

I have noted the remarkable evolution of the profession, from the nineteenth century westward migration-spawned railroad era to today's technology-focused efforts to provide assurance and advice that help manage risk in a complex and volatile world. Throughout, change has been an ever-present companion. However, the pace of change has been accelerating at every step along the way.

In *The Speed of Risk: Lessons Learned on the Audit Trail*, 2nd Edition, I consistently focused on the need for a more continuous approach to risk assessment and auditing at the speed of risk. I made the case that the accelerated pace at which new risks emerge and threaten make annual audit plans "relics of the past" that position internal auditors to address yesterday's challenges instead of today's.

Yet, much of the methodology on which we base our work has not changed much from when I began my own internal audit journey in 1975. Were it not for the use of technology, I would not be able to distinguish a lot of the methodologies from then to now. Given how little we have changed, it is not surprising that the perception of the profession by our stakeholders also has been slow to change. When I consider how we were seen back then — as the "corporate police" constantly churning out "gotcha" reports from cyclical audit plans — I wonder with some dread whether we are still seen that way in some circles.

Whether it is changing outdated processes and methodologies or correcting stakeholder misperceptions, we have much work to do before we can claim to be a profession of change agents. But sometimes the things that appear to hold us back can also hold the answers to our biggest needs.

One of our profession's greatest strengths is the methodical approach we take to our work. Indeed, part of the definition of internal auditing highlights this strength by describing us as bringing "a systematic, disciplined approach to evaluate and improve the effectiveness of risk management, control, and governance processes." One could make the case that this careful approach to our work also makes us reticent to make changes to our processes. However, nothing in the definition of internal audit precludes innovation, creativity, and imagination.

Appetite for Change

The modern internal auditor's use of statistical analysis, predictive analytics, behavioral psychology, RPA, Agile methodologies, and AI shows that embracing technology and novel approaches strengthens the profession's ability to provide assurance and advice on the effectiveness of risk management, control, and governance processes.

Yet, for too many internal audit functions, the use of more advanced processes is limited. What's more, there seems to be a limited appetite to routinely examine the effectiveness of how we do our work. A sampling of data from a recent *Pulse of Internal Audit* report reflects the low uptake of technology and slow updating of processes to keep pace with change:

- Less than half (45%) of CAEs consider their internal audit functions to be very or extremely agile.[2]
- Just 32% of CAEs strongly agree their internal audit functions challenge their own status quos.[3]
- Only 3 in 10 CAEs report they use advanced data analytics to identify and assess emerging or atypical risks.[4]

Despite those troubling statistics, we should take heart from the profession's history and its consistent ability to pivot to the needs of our organizations. We also should take note of the optimistic tone set by Shannon Urban, VP, CAE at Hasbro and a former IIA North American Board chairman, when discussing the need for innovation within the profession.

"Innovation in internal auditing is both crucial for its growth and necessary in meeting the ever-changing needs of stakeholders," she said. "It is a messy, frustrating, and ongoing program that demands commitment and courage. And it is fun, surprising, and rewarding. All auditors can take a few easy steps to start, or reboot, their journey today. If we want to understand our stakeholders and serve them well in the future, embracing innovation is the only option."[5]

At the same time, we also should heed the warning from the late U.S. President John F. Kennedy, who said, "There are risks and costs to a program of action. But they are far less than the long-range risks and costs of comfortable inaction."[6]

Four Areas in Need of Change

I've said it before: Change is difficult. Many of the issues addressed by Harvard Business School Professor Rosabeth Moss Kanter apply to the profession's reluctance to change: loss of control, excess uncertainty, concerns about competence, loss of face, and added work. However, to understand and better serve our stakeholders, as Shannon Urban urges, and to avoid the dangers of "comfortable inaction" that President Kennedy warned about, the profession must address the need for change in four key areas — processes, work products, skillsets, and mindsets.

Processes

It is important to understand that a process is simply a series of steps taken to achieve an end. When we recognize that many of the familiar routines we hold dear are simply steps in a series, we may find it easier to modify them or let them go altogether.

One area where process change has taken hold for the profession is the growing adoption of Agile work methodologies. The Agile process is adapted from Agile software development, which describes the use of specific agile software development methodologies and an associated mindset shift to achieve more value and agility from the internal audit process.[7] *Agile Auditing: Transforming the Internal Audit Process* by Rick A. Wright, Jr., published by the Internal Audit Foundation, provides an excellent in-depth examination of Agile internal auditing. Wright makes the distinction in his book between what he describes as little "a" agile and big "A" agile. The latter addresses the specific Agile process. Little "a" describes process improvement efforts to achieve a more nimble, less wasteful internal auditing process.[8] In my view, it is the little "a" that holds the greatest potential to transform our profession. We explore developing a little "a" agile mindset and the use of big "A" Agile auditing in chapter 5, "Driving Change Means Being Agile."

Another insight that supports process change is to separate process from how we define our value. This requires having a clear understanding of what we do.

Work Product

When it comes to how and what we do, the discussion should begin with defining our work product. Here's a shocker: The audit report is not our work product any more than a cereal box is the work product of a cereal maker. The audit report is simply the packaging. Timely, accurate, reliable, and relevant delivery of information to our stakeholders is our product.

Let's take a moment to consider the value of our work product. Organizations are under constant pressure to recognize, leverage, and manage risk to help carry out strategies and achieve goals. Having a clear understanding of the risk landscape and the likelihood and impact of those risks on the organization is imperative. This is how the work we do — providing assurance and advice on the effectiveness of risk management, control, and governance processes — adds value.

However, we must consider that our stakeholders — boards and executive management — must balance a multitude of competing and intertwined interests and priorities. They are constantly barraged with information from myriad sources. If we insist on burying timely, reliable, and relevant information in lengthy reports, we quickly run the risk of becoming *irrelevant*. This insight takes on added significance in the current environment where dynamic risks, environmental, economic and political volatility, and disruptive innovation demand that our stakeholders have the right information at the right time.

Despite that, many practitioners continue to rely on established processes and focus on capturing every trifling detail in their reports. The profession's approach to workpapers is an ideal example of why we must rethink how we develop and deliver our core product. Chapter 5 explores how an agile mindset can enhance the internal audit reporting process. But the timeliness battle is often lost before the reporting process has even begun. One way we impair our performance is by how we document our work.

As a young internal auditor, I took very seriously the painstaking art of documenting the results of my internal audit work in workpapers. I believed that well-organized, comprehensive workpapers were critical to demonstrating the quality of my efforts, and that they were the basis for the audit report I would write at the conclusion of the audit.

I understood that the workpapers needed to include documentation of evidence I examined, and that the evidence needed to be relevant, reliable, sufficient, and useful. I adapted to the culture of the profession of the time. And I came to believe that internal audit workpapers were good, and more workpapers were better.

When I rose to the level of a CAE, my perspective on workpapers changed dramatically. I was determined to achieve greater efficiencies in the department, enhance our capacity to audit more risks, and add value for the organization. I undertook a complete review of our internal audit processes and identified many opportunities for improvement. One area in which we were woefully inefficient was in the conduct of our audits — particularly in the documentation of our audit results in the workpapers.

As I reviewed more of our audits, I came to refer to much of what was included as "happy workpapers." These were packed with evidence that everything was fine; documents that merely confirmed that controls were adequately designed and implemented. When everything an internal auditor encounters during the course of an audit is simply captured and included in the workpapers, they soon can be measured in linear feet.

The IIA's *Standards* are appropriately flexible when prescribing documentation requirements. Following are the two most relevant passages:

> Standard 2310 – Identifying Information: "Internal auditors must identify sufficient, reliable, relevant, and useful information to achieve the engagement's objectives."
>
> Standard 2330 – Documenting Information: "Internal auditors must document sufficient, reliable, relevant, and useful information to support the engagement results and conclusions."[9]

The IIA offers additional insight when considering sufficiency: "Sufficient information is factual, adequate, and convincing so that a prudent informed person would reach the same conclusion as the auditor."

I am particularly partial to guidance provided in U.S. Government Auditing Standards (the Yellow Book), which offers the following to government auditors on what should be included when documenting evidence in workpapers:

> 8.135.b. "the work performed and evidence obtained to support significant judgments and conclusions, as well as expectations in analytical procedures, including descriptions of transactions and records examined (for example, by listing file numbers, case numbers, or other means of identifying specific documents examined, **though copies of documents examined or detailed listings of information from those documents are not required**)"[10] (emphasis added).

Every internal audit department should have a system of controls that ensures the quality of audit results. Any that struggle with the timeliness should seriously consider these policies with an eye toward becoming more agile and relevant.

Skillsets

One of the biggest challenges to internal auditing posed by the rapid advance of technology is keeping our skillsets relevant to the needs of our organizations. Auditing cybersecurity comes to mind as one of the most important risks that organizations face in the twenty-first century.

For the better part of a decade, protecting organizations from cyber threats has consistently ranked as a top risk for organizations. Yet, the profession continues to struggle with having the right talent on staff to effectively audit this risk. Data from a recent *Pulse of Internal Audit* report provides a snapshot of how challenging this risk has become.

"Pulse data reflect potentially significant 'effort gaps' when it comes to providing assurance over key areas of cybersecurity. The gap is defined as the difference between the level of effort the internal audit function currently delivers in a particular area versus how much the function should provide, as determined by respondents."[11]

- CAEs report a 36% gap between actual vs. desired assurance over readiness and response to cyber threats.[12]
- 51% of CAEs cite lack of cyber expertise on staff as an obstacle to addressing cybersecurity risk.[13]

In my blog, *Chambers on the Profession*, I offered predictions for the 2020s, two of which are appropriate to this discussion. From "The Road Ahead for Internal Audit: 5 Bold Predictions for the 2020s":

The rise of "Uber" auditing. The "gig economy" — a labor market characterized by the prevalence of short-term contracts or freelance work, as opposed to permanent jobs — will find a natural fit in internal auditing. The demand for tech-savvy internal audit professionals who can skillfully respond to cyber threats and other technology-related risks already outpaces supply. This will make it increasingly attractive for practitioners with these skills and others to offer their services through short-term, on-demand contracts.

From the chief audit executive's perspective, sourcing strategies will include on-demand professionals. There will soon come a time when it will make more sense to simply call a service or turn to an app that will help locate the needed short-term expert to complete an internal audit engagement or advisory project.

The torch will be passed to a new tech-savvy and tech-fearless generation. *Internal Auditor* magazine recently featured its annual list of Emerging Leaders, and reading the profiles of these young dreamers is like peering through a window into the future.

Their embrace of data analytics, robotics, and blockchain technology is a given. Many not only understand technology but are adept at writing code and designing data-analytics programs. This diverse, multinational group recognizes the value of integrating technology into audit and governance strategies. The most encouraging aspect of this development is that embracing technology is what will best position the next generation of internal auditors to remain trusted advisors.[14]

We all must embrace the zeal displayed by the *Internal Auditor* Emerging Leaders and eagerly build new skillsets that correspond to a constantly changing risk landscape. For the profession overall, it is imperative that we understand that needed skillsets must continue to evolve to match changing risks. To keep pace with changing demands on our skillsets, as well as process and work product, we will need to change our mindset.

Mindset

The common thread that runs through the first three topics — process, work products, and skillsets — is embracing a mindset for change. Beyond thinking about how we audit and what we audit, we must examine why we audit.

The mission of internal audit is simple and clear: *To enhance and protect organizational value by providing risk-based and objective assurance, advice, and insight.* If our work is indeed to *enhance* and *protect*, we must be prepared to *adapt* to new risks areas and the new demands on our skills that come with them.

Kenneth Chen, vice president and chief audit executive at Spotify, has built a 25-member team on the premise that helping the organization succeed is fundamental to internal audit's job. Indeed, the function's motto, "Enable growth and protect value by providing insights to anticipate and navigate risks," embraces the change agent attitude. For Spotify, internal audit is the voice in the room supporting growth and innovation while reminding people there is value that must be protected.

"It's about selling the story of the benefit we can bring to the table. It's why we should be at the table and not an afterthought," Chen said in an interview with Deloitte's *Resilient* podcast.[15] "It's why we can help them be successful in their market launch or in their product launch. It's asking those difficult questions that they may not actually have ever thought about and then telling them why it matters to them."

Chen's description of his team's work sounds typical for a progressive internal audit function, but the devil is in the details. For example, his teams are mapped to individual business units to ensure constant communication, which includes quarterly meetings with department heads to update risk assessments. This investment is critical to being viewed as a partner within the organization.

"Spotify is a lot like other tech companies. What happened last quarter is a distant memory. We have to keep updated on strategic projects," he said. "A huge part of the reason we work this way is to integrate ourselves into the business units, understand what they're working on, and help them address risks along the way. If I want to go against the grain on a particular project, I need to provide real-time value that is relevant and to the point."

This approach flips the old internal audit approach of only going to the business unit to "check up" on their work, Chen said. Instead, internal audit at Spotify is driven by helping the company get it right the first time.

"I need to be a relevant party," he said. "How do I connect the dots to help you get where you're going? One of my objectives is to provide assurance, but I'm also there to help Spotify succeed."

This mindset is fundamental not just to protecting value but to enhancing and creating value.

Chen's success story at Spotify is built on what he refers to as "selling" the story of internal audit's value to the organization. As he notes, "It's why we should be at the table and not an afterthought." Based on the survey for *Agents of Change*, that message is getting through to many of our stakeholders.

Nearly half (46%) of the CAEs who responded to the survey believe their board/audit committee is fully supportive of internal audit acting as a change agent. If you add those who believe boards are moderately supportive, the figure jumps to 80%. The findings are equally encouraging for executive management, where 76% of responding CAEs believe executive management is fully or moderately supportive (see **exhibit 4-1**).

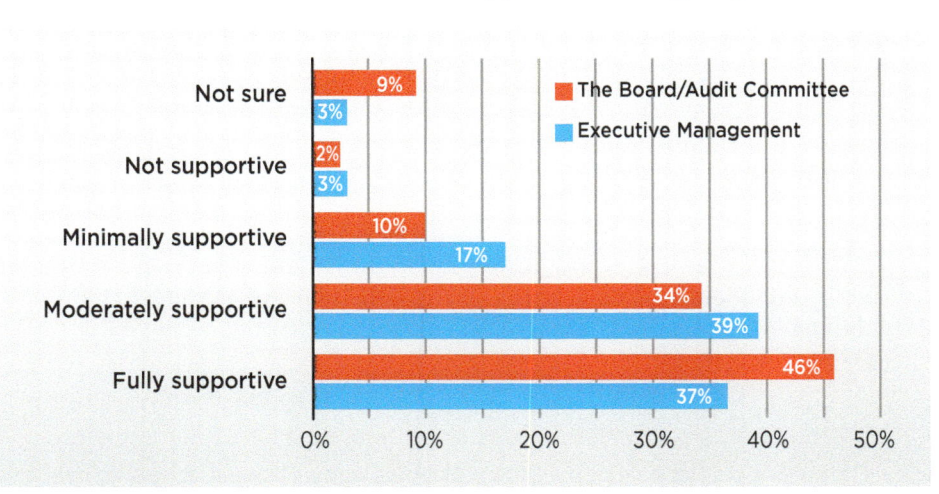

Exhibit 4-1: Stakeholder Support for Change Agents

	The Board/Audit Committee	Executive Management
Not sure	9%	3%
Not supportive	2%	3%
Minimally supportive	10%	17%
Moderately supportive	34%	39%
Fully supportive	46%	37%

Note: Q7-8: What is X's position on internal audit driving change within your organization? n = 606

So, what is holding us back? The survey provides some insights into that question. While more than three-quarters of CAEs believe they have moderate to full support to act as value creators within their organizations, only half believe their internal audit functions are viewed as agents of change (see **exhibit 4-2**).

Exhibit 4-2: Few Internal Audit Functions Viewed as Agents of Change

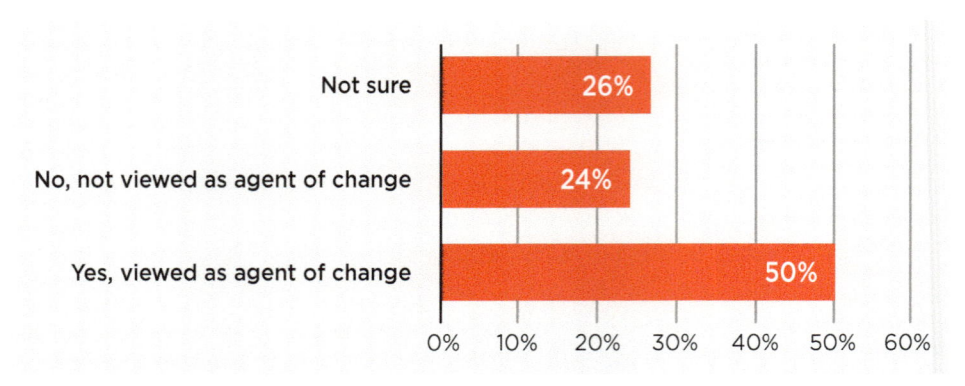

Response	Percentage
Not sure	26%
No, not viewed as agent of change	24%
Yes, viewed as agent of change	50%

Note: Q9: Is the internal audit function within your organization viewed as an Agent of Change? n = 606

To close the gap, we must begin by forging a culture of change within internal audit that embraces the change-agent mindset.

Developing a Culture of Change

Managing and swaying culture within an organization is challenging. There are many influencing factors, internally and externally. Tone at the top — the messages both overt and covert put out by leaders — is the most talked about, but there are other dimensions. The profession's recent foray into auditing culture provides insight to help us look at culture within our internal audit functions.

One clear and early lesson on auditing culture is understanding that what is done is more important than what is said. In *The Speed of Risk,* I devoted a chapter to auditing culture. One key takeaway was that understanding what culture is — and isn't — is critical.

> "One definition describes culture as the 'moral fabric' of the organization. Another describes it as 'the self-sustaining pattern of behavior that determines how things are done.' I tend to prefer a much simpler definition: Culture is 'how we do things around here.'

This short phrase packs a big punch as much for what it says as what it doesn't say. It's important to understand that culture is defined by the actual day-to-day operations, interactions, and influences within an organization, not what a mission statement, CEO speech, or employee policy manual says it is. Culture is not what is said; it's what is done."

This is particularly apropos when discussing culture within an internal audit department. For years we have been talking about becoming more agile and flexible, improving communications with stakeholders, embracing technology, and updating processes. Yet, for all the talk, actions and real change have been slow to follow.

Too many internal audit functions are content to operate in a safe and familiar environment. But we must recognize that the purpose of an audit engagement is not to simply point out errors, or cause an impact and then make recommendations on how to not do it again. That has limited value. While it protects value, it rarely enhances or adds value.

Truly innovative and dynamic audit departments are constantly reinventing the way they do things. CAEs must set a tone at the top that embraces and nurtures innovation and change. That starts with internal audit's own strategic plan, which must be forward-looking and provide a roadmap for needed change within internal audit.

I have long asserted that the biggest strategic risk for internal audit functions, and even the profession itself, is complacency. From my experience, success more often begets complacency than more success. The CAE change agents in our profession are restless visionaries who strive for their departments to drive needed change in the organization. They work constantly to improve and enhance the internal audit function, and are never content to "do things the way they have always been done."

These CAEs drive their internal audit functions to be agile, flexible, and willing to embrace change — subtle or radical — depending on the risks and the needs of the organization. If you are not willing to change your approaches and processes, it's unlikely you will ever be an agent of change. The agile mindset says, "I'm going to do what I need to do to deliver answers in time to make a difference."

CHAPTER 5
Driving Change Means Being Agile

— • • • • —

Life is either a daring adventure or nothing. To keep our faces toward change and behave like free spirits in the presence of fate is strength undefeatable.

— Helen Keller —

The word agility gets used a lot these days. In recent years, it has been infused into the mainstream vocabulary of the internal audit profession. Books and articles abound on "agile auditing." It would be difficult to find an internal audit conference where at least one presenter isn't speaking on agile auditing. So why has agility become such an imperative? I believe it's because of where we find ourselves and where we as a profession aspire to go. I believe that for agents of change, disruption, change, and agility are inextricability linked.

As I prepared to write this chapter, I was struck by the fact that I have actually been espousing agility for our profession for more than 25 years. Agility became an imperative for the first major audit leadership assignment in my career as director of the U.S. Army's Worldwide Internal Review Program. I shared my experiences in leading that organization through transformation in my first book, *Lessons Learned on the Audit Trail*. But, in the context of agility, it's worth a deeper dive here.

A Case Study in Agility

In the early 1990s, the long-simmering Cold War between the west and former Soviet-bloc countries suddenly ended. In the United States, the words "peace dividend" quickly emerged, signaling a strong desire by taxpayers and political leaders to reduce the heavy burden of defense expenditures that had been perceived as necessary for decades. As an internal auditor in the U.S. Army, I began to quickly see the consequences of reduced budgets on military operations and readiness that were often the focus of our audit plans. It didn't take long before the spending cuts began to directly impact the budgets of our internal audit departments.

It was during this period of disruptive budget reductions that I assumed the role as the Army's director of internal review based at the Pentagon. While I was honored to take on such an important post, I felt a little like the captain of the Titanic right after it hit the iceberg. In the five years before then, budgets at internal review offices worldwide had reduced the total size of staff from 2,100 to 1,400. The Army overall hadn't shrunk by one-third, yet internal audit resources were frequent targets. Some departments were reduced by 75%, and others eliminated altogether.

At the encouragement of Army leadership, I undertook an extensive study to understand better why internal audit's stakeholders were pulling the plug on us. I traveled around the world, visiting about two dozen offices. At each location, I would sit down with senior military executives to understand where internal audit was falling short and why it was seen as so expendable. The insights I gained from those conversations have stuck with me to this day.

I learned that internal audit was being drastically reduced because its stakeholders didn't feel we added value at a time when they had to make tough budget decisions. Specifically:

- Internal audit wasn't focused on the real risks its organization faced.
- Internal audit's reports often didn't offer meaningful solutions.
- Internal audits took too long and frequently delivered information too late.
- Internal audit reports were often long-winded and difficult for busy leaders to digest.

As I chronicled in *The Speed of Risk*, the feedback was eye-opening:

> "You know, those guys come in and tell me what I already know," some of them said. Others responded, "They tell me things are broken, but I already know they are broken. *I need somebody who can tell me how to fix them.*" Conversely, more than once I heard this: "Sometimes I only need to know 'what time it is,' but the internal review guys insist on giving me voluminous reports that tell me 'how to build the watch.'"[1]

The outcome of my study was a call to action for our worldwide team. We knew we needed to move swiftly and decisively to address the weaknesses exposed in our approach. In short, we had to be willing to change our audit processes so that we would become perpetually agile in the way we delivered our services.

Our stakeholders were telling us unequivocally that the scope audits we had been performing — evaluating an entire department or system or activity — were not what they needed. They considered them laborious, cumbersome, and time-consuming, and they didn't find the final reports to be very useful. Our rigid planning cycles and inflexible audit policies were culprits that drove audit cycle time (the time it took to complete an audit) to weeks and months when decisions had to be made in days.

Stakeholders considered us to be too focused on compliance issues and not focused enough on ways to help them improve the efficiency and effectiveness of their operations. They viewed many of our audits as irrelevant, not focused on the biggest risks then facing the Army, and not relating to the key issues being discussed and debated throughout the organization.

As I noted in *The Speed of Risk*:

> "Excessive overhead had become a problem, and the quality of our work had suffered. I noted that some internal review offices had been downsized in such a way that they were top-heavy with management and administration. I remember a department that at one time had five staff — a chief or director, a secretary, and three audit staff. Two positions were eliminated — a 40% reduction — but the cuts had been allowed to occur through attrition, so when two of the three audit staffers departed, the department was left with one chief, one secretary, and one auditor. In effect, the department had absorbed a 66% reduction in internal audit capability, rather than 40%.

One commander (CEO) noted that he had spent almost $1 million on the department the previous year yet had received only five reports. Although the number of reports really shouldn't be used to determine the value received, clearly in his mind there was a correlation."

We had our work cut out for us, but failure to address the feedback was not an option. Working with regional internal audit leaders from around the world, we set out to transform internal review into a leaner, more efficient audit organization that delivered timely and accurate information to executives in time to make decisions. In other words, we had to become more agile so we could move "quickly and easily" to serve our organizations. But this was years before the more formal approach to "Agile auditing" was introduced. Instead, we leveraged an "agile mindset" to drive the needed transformation.

Faced with the loss of stakeholder confidence and other daunting challenges, we embraced an agile mindset and deployed the little "a" agile internal auditing process described in chapter 4. We transformed ourselves to achieve a strategic vision of being *"the premiere source of information for the Army's decision-makers."*

Our objectives were to execute our mission smarter, faster, and with more impactful results. We developed strategies around people, processes, and technology. The key features of our "reengineered" approach included:

- Deploying a staff sourcing strategy that included full-time, contract, and guest auditors.
- Transforming the audit planning process so that it centered on crisp, clear, and concise objectives as opposed to those that were broad and open-ended.
- Adopting audit methodologies that leveraged state-of-the art technologies of the time and deemphasized extensive unnecessary documentation and review.
- Streamlining audit reporting processes focused on timely delivery of the final audit report.

Our quest for greater agility to serve the needs of our customers delivered remarkable results. In less than four years, we reduced the average cycle time for internal audit engagements Army-wide from 56 days to only 14. We enhanced our return on investment — in this case, the cost of operations versus identified, agreed-to savings. As we measured it, our ROI jumped from 3-to-1 to an astounding 24-to-1.

The number of audit engagements completed worldwide doubled over the same period to more than 4,400. Although downsizing continued throughout the Army, internal review no longer shrank at a disproportionate rate.

I view agile auditing much like I do enterprise risk management. It's not as critical that you embrace a formal framework or structured approach, such as "Agile" auditing. It's more important that you leverage an agile mindset to constantly strive for efficiency and be able to pivot swiftly in executing the internal audit mission. Our journey was the right one for us under the circumstances, but today many internal audit functions are embracing big "A" Agile internal auditing. And the results can be quite impressive.

Agile Auditing

As we discuss throughout this book, the twenty-first century has brought new challenges and opportunities for the internal audit profession. The speed of risk has increased exponentially, and traditional internal audit methodologies have struggled to enable the profession to keep pace. The emergence of Agile auditing has offered promise to the profession. A recent survey of more than 1,000 internal auditors by software provider AuditBoard revealed that 82% believe Agile auditing "has the potential to add more value to their work compared to the traditional project approach — although 45% reported a lack of knowledge resources as the most significant obstacle to adopting Agile."[2]

Aaron Wright, AuditBoard director of audit solutions, succinctly summarizes Agile auditing in a recent whitepaper:

> Agile is a term that's used to describe a set of principles and methodologies that were initially formed for use in software development and popularized by the Agile Manifesto for Software Development in 2001. This included four values below and 12 principles that focus on delivering value. The values shown here recognize that, while all elements are needed, those in **bold** should take precedence over those *italicized*.
>
> 1. **Individuals and interactions** over *processes and tools.*
> 2. **Working software** over *comprehensive documentation.*
> 3. **Customer collaboration** over *contract negotiation.*
> 4. **Responding to change** over *following a plan.*

Agile allows project teams to focus on delivering value, and acknowledges that the traditional "heavy" project management methodologies (namely, Waterfall) follow a linear process that often slows teams down. "Agile" in and of itself is not a process framework, but rather a general term describing a collection of "light" project management frameworks — Scrum and Kanban being the most popular.

Since their inception to common knowledge as a result of the manifesto nearly two decades ago, agile methodologies have been adopted in virtually every business sector, including auditing. As auditors, we love nothing more than processes and comprehensive documentation — and while adopting agile ways of working may cause a bit of panic initially, it can provide numerous benefits.[3]

The concept of developing a customized "Agile Manifesto" for those internal audit departments that seek to adopt Agile auditing is a great idea. In a recent whitepaper, Deloitte encourages creation of a manifesto that is "aspirational as well as practical. As one of the first efforts in adopting the methodology, the exercise of developing the manifesto may be more valuable than the manifesto itself."[4]

Deloitte offers an "Internal Audit Agile Manifesto" for consideration by those contemplating adoption of the methodology. It includes nine elements:

1. Outcome-driven | Value-driven
2. Just-in-time | Proactive approach to the "right projects at the right depth/focus"
3. One size does not fit all — customized project focused on value and risk
4. Collaborative approach — take the journey with our clients
5. Mix it up a little bit, break some eggs — challenge "That's the way we've always done it."
6. Decisioning "as you go" with transparency and alignment
7. Continuous communication with all stakeholders
8. Be quick and iterative versus confined to a plan
9. Impact over thoroughness — "good enough" (80/20 rule)[5]

As Deloitte notes, the manifesto should not be set in stone. Those deploying Agile auditing should add, delete, or modify elements of their manifesto as they become more experienced with it.[6]

Features of Agile Auditing

There is no authoritative source that prescribes required features of Agile auditing. Instead, as noted earlier, it subscribes broadly to the Agile Manifesto for Software Development. However, there are common features that are emerging in the adoption of Agile auditing. Rick Wright provides an overview in his book:

> **"Focus on value rather than audit objectives.** Agile IA (internal audit) engagements define the value to be sought from the engagement up front. This helps ensure the focus throughout the audit engagement is on the goal of producing value for the organization by aligning audit deliverables with strategies and objectives of the organization. Traditional waterfall audits tend to focus on identifying audit objectives during the planning phase, which may or may not result in optimization of value that is generated from the engagement. The focus on audit objectives implies the audit engagement derives value from itself. For instance, an audit objective might be "to ensure controls are effectively executed." On the surface there is nothing inherently wrong with this objective as stated. However, as stated, this audit objective is merely looking to see if a control is executed properly and may not consider whether it helps to achieve the organization's business goals. Consequently, the value of this effort is dependent on the assumption that controls have intrinsic value, when in fact they may not.
>
> **Client involvement.** In some iterations of Agile IA, audit clients are invited to be an integral part of the engagement project team. This greatly enhances communication between parties because there is more frequent audit client interaction throughout the engagement lifecycle. Complex projects can benefit tremendously from the subject matter expertise the audit client may offer the project team. This feature is incorporated by design into mature Agile IA implementations.
>
> **Time-boxed discipline.** Time boxes are fixed length work cycles usually measured in weeks. Because Agile IA engagements are completed in a series of incremental workflows that are time boxed, there is built-in discipline for planning and completing audit tasks on time. This greatly

reduces the risk of audit engagement budget overruns and enhances the audit team focus.

Timely insights and risk responses. When audit clients are made a part of the engagement team, they are walking the audit journey side by side with the audit team as work is completed. This means audit clients are also getting real-time feedback on audit results and corresponding insights. Rather than audit insights being delayed while results are validated (as in traditional waterfall audits), audit clients can begin formulating responses to risk right away.

Point-of-view insights vs. fact-focused findings. Agile IA values the process of learning throughout the engagement. This allows for the audit team to develop points of view about the audit subject that go beyond mere findings of fact. Points of view are audit insights that may express data-driven opinions and thought-provoking ideas for audit client consideration that align audit observations with business strategies or other bigger picture themes. This contrasts with the sometimes excessively cleansed audit findings typical of the traditional waterfall audit approach (i.e., because audit clients are more intimately involved in the Agile IA process, there is less opportunity, and perceived need, for this excessive cleansing to take place). In the waterfall audit scenario, engagement observations are tethered to the limited scope of the audit objectives. Additionally, audit management who are responsible for performing audit engagement reviews may lack intimate familiarity with the nuances of the engagement findings possessed by audit team staff who performed the work, further leading to watered down audit insights.

Fewer disagreements on results between audit team and audit client. Because audit clients are more intimately engaged as an Agile IA engagement progresses, there are opportunities for audit results to be discussed, mutually vetted, and agreed upon concurrently with the audit team. This feature of Agile IA can greatly reduce the potential for disagreements in audit conclusions at the end of an audit engagement. Additionally, because audit clients may be involved in the discovery process of reaching audit conclusions, there is greater likelihood that audit clients will fully embrace audit results and take stronger ownership positions toward responses.

Documentation rationalization. A key principle of Agile software development (Agile SD) advocates for simplicity (i.e., the art of maximizing the amount of work not done). This is a powerful idea for making the audit process more efficient. Workpaper documentation is a potential area of significant waste in traditional waterfall audit methodology. The amount of extraneous documentation that has found a mainstream footing in traditional audit engagements can be overwhelming and frustrating to audit staff, and often adds little or no incremental value. Agile IA challenges a common myth that more is better in regard to documentation, as well as other areas of waste in the audit cycle."[7]

The Benefits of Agile Auditing

The benefits of Agile auditing are quickly apparent, even in the preceding basic examination of its features. Chief among them are speed and responsiveness. As traditional waterfall methodologies are shelved for Agile methodologies, internal audit teams are discovering that many of the obstacles to auditing at the speed of risk become less daunting. Without being siloed into rigid teams or processes, AuditBoard's Aaron Wright notes at least six key benefits that can be achieved:

- "**Less time spent on planning the audit:** This could mean shaving a one- or two-month-long planning phase down to a week or a few days.

- **Combining all planning, fieldwork, and reporting elements:** Agile's short, time-boxed iterations of work (commonly referred to as 'sprints') enable audit teams to incorporate these project phases together, eliminating disparity from one phase to the next.

- **Increased customer interaction:** Agile sprints facilitate weekly or even daily customer interaction and engagement. The traditional waterfall approach makes communication with stakeholders more limited and infrequent.

- **Changing audit focus and updating scope:** Agile allows internal audit an opportunity to update the audit scope or even modify the audit's focus altogether based on newly available information — with appropriate levels of approval, of course.

- **Sharing findings and starting remediation:** Through increased customer interaction, final audit report results and findings are shared with stakeholders as they emerge — instead of waiting for the end of the audit closing meeting.

- **Abbreviating the audit plan:** This means putting the emphasis on the quarter rather than on the year — and homing in on what's coming up in the next three months as compared to the next nine to 12 months."[8]

As Agile auditing has gained popularity, there have been some misconceptions about it within the internal audit profession. In another whitepaper on the subject, aptly titled "Auditing Agile Projects: Your Grandfather's Audit Won't Work Here!," Deloitte notes:

> Common to these misconceptions is the belief that Agile projects are somehow "free-for-alls" that lack any type of rigor or formal processes — something that is guaranteed to make them more risky than traditional software development initiatives and throw a monkey wrench into any attempt to audit them. Yet, the reality is quite the opposite. Agile projects present the same inherent risks as traditional projects. What differs is the Agile process itself and, therefore, how risks are addressed and mitigated. For that reason, as auditors, IA teams need to take a step back and switch lenses — and as with Agile projects themselves, teams need to adopt a different approach.[9]

The Future of Agile Auditing

Agile auditing has definitely gained traction in recent years, yet even its most ardent proponents acknowledge that only a small percentage of internal audit functions have adopted big "A" Agile auditing. I fervently believe the profession needs to embrace the type of change being promoted by Agile audit enthusiasts. Yet, based on my experience, I believe the rate of adoption will be slow. Internal auditors are, by nature, risk-averse. Agile auditing will resonate with a broad cross-section of the profession only when its benefits are fully appreciated — and when it is being widely promoted by The IIA and others whose voices are influential.

Regardless of the rate of adoption of Agile auditing, there are imperatives for internal audit functions striving to be change agents that are even more critical. One such imperative is a strong reliance on technology to facilitate the audit process. This is a topic that we will explore in more depth in the next chapter.

CHAPTER 6
Leveraging Enabling Technology

— • • • • —

When in doubt, choose change.

— Lily Leung —

As we have explored, internal auditors must have an agile mindset to be effective agents of change. That agile mindset must drive innovation, either through informal or formal transformation of audit processes. But transformation of manual processes alone rarely produces the impact that change agents must deliver. To be powerful change agents, internal auditors must also be tech-savvy and tech-fearless, and leveraging IT starts with the use of enabling technology in the internal audit function itself.

In my 12 years as president and CEO of The IIA, I witnessed firsthand how technology evolved to better serve those in our profession who strive to be agents of change. Advancements in data analytics, audit automation software, robotics process automation (RPA), and artificial intelligence (AI) technology, as well as the industry's embrace of Agile auditing methodologies and principles, have enabled audit teams to perform their jobs more efficiently, accurately, and strategically. Frankly, innovation has become essential to helping internal auditors effectively provide the assurance and advisory services required of their roles.

This is especially valuable because events such as the COVID-19 crisis, the ever-growing threats of cyber risk, social unrest, and economic uncertainty have placed increased pressure on internal audit functions to become more dynamic and agile to help their organizations manage these and other risks. Periods of dynamic risk have brought with them challenges, including enabling a distributed workforce, helping organizations identify and address new and emerging risks, and supporting efforts to meet shifting compliance requirements.

Yet, technological advancements alone won't help internal audit effectively adapt to new conditions and overcome obstacles; it takes internal auditors with a change-agent mindset to advocate for adoption of technology that can help them drive valuable outcomes. There are many internal audit teams that have dramatically enhanced performance using technology. A good example is United Bankshares (UBSI), a $19.7 billion regional bank holding company with dual headquarters in Washington, DC, and Charleston, West Virginia. From 2011 to 2017, the company completed four significant acquisitions that more than doubled its asset size. Tasked with rapidly scaling their audit program to cover new areas, aligning with new regulatory requirements and audit quality standards, and keeping pace with the company's growth, UBSI's senior internal audit manager and her internal audit managers realized it was time to seek a better organized, user-friendly software platform for their 26-member team.

UBSI's internal audit leadership successfully advocated for making a change that streamlined formal audit procedures through automation, optimized coordination between internal audit and its stakeholders, and scaled their Sarbanes-Oxley 404 control suite. That freed up time and resources to address new risk areas associated with the company's growth while reducing internal audit's budget by 35% a year. Those efficiencies and cost savings were achieved by switching from an older tool to a flexible, cloud-based solution called AuditBoard that could grow with their audit program.

UBSI nicely illustrates audit leaders who embrace a change-agent mindset by leveraging technology to create value for their business. Yet, while UBSI's success story is inspiring, it is a disturbingly rare scenario among internal audit departments.

In this chapter, I examine internal audit's long-simmering love/hate relationship with technology, including diving into the history of technology adoption. I describe critical areas where I believe technology is crucial for building a change-enabling foundation and discuss what to look for in first-rate solutions that empower auditors to be agents of change.

Staying the Course: Is It Worth It?

Internal audit functions must keep pace with the speed of the organizations they serve. Yet, recent research suggests that internal audit lags other departments when it comes to adopting automation software to streamline their day-to-day audit activities, such as planning, fieldwork, issue management, and reporting to the audit committee and board. A recent IIA survey of more than 500 U.S. and Canadian internal audit leaders found that, while more than a third of respondents reported increased use of emerging technologies such as data analytics and Agile auditing techniques, a mere 12% reported increased investment in automation software.[1]

Yet, in less than a generation, automation software has become synonymous with doing business. The list of examples is long and familiar: Netsuite (accounting); Workday and ADP (human resources and payroll); Salesforce (sales); Atlassian (engineering and project management); Zendesk (customer service); and Hubspot and Marketo (marketing). These cloud-based solutions have dominated their respective industries not only because they are effective collaboration platforms, but because they are specifically designed to help create efficiencies through organization and automation of day-to-day department processes.

In contrast, the go-to "solution" for far too many audit functions remains spreadsheets, email, shared drives, and homegrown tools. The greatest drawback to this approach is the large amount of administrative work that auditors must perform to manage their audit projects. Valuable time is lost to manual, repetitive activities and reconciling version-control issues, not to mention that a decentralized control environment often leads to a lack of visibility, inefficiencies, and redundancies in activities among audit, risk, and compliance groups.

One rarely discussed reason why the industry has been slow to adopt automation software is that purpose-built audit automation technology didn't begin hitting its stride until recent years. Prior to that, traditional governance, risk, and compliance solutions were the primary options available to audit departments. While those solutions were designed for use by the C-suite with optimized dashboards and reports, they were not built to automate audit lifecycle processes or improve on-the-job collaboration for auditors and their stakeholders. In the past five years, a new breed of solutions has begun to proliferate with deeper domain expertise, focus on user experience, and higher engagement and collaboration by audit users and their stakeholders. They are designed to automate the administrative activities essential to the auditor's day-to-day work by centralizing all internal audit data in one reliable location that acts as the single "source of truth." The capabilities of these new solutions far exceed those of spreadsheets and the older technologies, with departments that successfully implement them reporting time savings of 33% to 50% on administrative audit work performed during testing and documentation.[2]

Using Technology to Reengineer Internal Audit Processes

In *The Speed of Risk*, I made the case that excessive cycle times lead to outdated results, which diminish internal audit's value and lead to stakeholder dissatisfaction. I identified five internal audit processes as key candidates for reengineering: risk assessments, audit planning, documentation and review, reporting, and monitoring and follow-up.

When managed manually, these processes are neither efficient nor cost-effective. Yet, the majority of a staff auditor's workload at any given time consists of some combination of these activities. It stands to reason that strategies to improve these activities through automation software and emerging technologies such as RPA and AI are *capacity multipliers*. In other words, the hours saved multiply an auditor's capacity to take on new projects. The extent to which auditors can employ technology to eliminate administrative activities and shorten the audit lifecycle frees them to work on projects of greater value to the business.

Let's look deeper into emerging technologies to understand how they can create greater efficiency, effectiveness, and value-add capacity for internal audit and the business.

Audit Management Software Helps Add Value

Audit management solutions, also known as audit automation solutions, help streamline workflows. At its core, cloud-based audit management software is a true digital system of record that unifies audit data in one place. Having a single, reliable source of data is foundational to begin automating processes that save valuable resource hours. I will explore this from the perspective of the audit processes that I believe are key candidates for reengineering:

> **Risk assessment.** PwC's recent *State of the Internal Audit Profession* study reveals that today's audit, risk, and compliance executives almost universally agree that annual plans and annual assessments are antiquated.[3] The most effective risk assessments are the ones that are continuous in nature. In an ever-evolving risk landscape, more frequent risk assessments help organizations stay on top of key risks, especially during

critical times of crisis, such as the COVID-19 pandemic, when audit leaders reported they were performing quarterly and even monthly risk assessments. Audit management software helps automate the distribution and aggregation of risk surveys, as well as the scoring process, saving considerable time for auditors and making it easier to deploy risk assessments more frequently. Software with suitable underlying architecture will link real-time risk data collected from risk assessments to controls and action plans throughout the platform.

Audit planning. In a dynamic risk environment, audit leaders are more frequently changing their audit plans throughout the year. The key features of an efficient and effective engagement-planning process include:

- Ensuring that risk assessment is the primary basis for determining objectives, scope, and specific tests.
- Using a sound and consistent methodology.
- Leveraging expertise from subject matter experts.
- Incorporating advice from management and operating personnel.
- Designing each engagement for efficiency, keeping the budget in mind.

Audit management software can facilitate the planning process by allowing audit teams to manage and collaborate on their audit plans and allocate resources in one place, driven by real-time risk assessment data that live within the same platform. The centralized nature of audit management software can provide auditors with flexibility to make changes to their audit plan quickly and to see those changes updated in real time. As audits progress, managers have real-time visibility into the status of their audit plan and can see how it tracks against department timelines and goals.

Documentation and review. In a manual environment, evidence management entails hours of reaching out to business owners and following up over email. A best practice is for these processes to follow a sound and documented methodology, rather than exist scattered across computers, emails, and differing versions. Audit management software stores all relevant audit documentation in one place, as well as automating its collection, updating, and reviewing processes, saving auditors time and effort.

Reporting. Audit management software is inherently equipped to help auditors provide stakeholders with more insights through real-time dashboards and reporting. With all audit data in one place, internal auditors are empowered to create reports more efficiently and produce useful insights more efficiently than in a manual reporting environment.

Monitoring and follow-up. Inefficient issue management can tally up hundreds of ill-spent hours for internal auditors. Audit management software enables auditors to streamline the issue management process, from identifying issues to follow-up and reporting. One feature to look for is remediation workflows with automated notifications, which can help internal auditors save time in closing out issues.

The activities described above are scenarios that are supported by quality audit automation software. Later in this chapter, I will discuss what to look for in such software solutions and whether it is the right route for your internal audit team.

Technology Is Essential to Agility

As I noted in chapter 5, the vast majority of internal auditors believe Agile auditing has the potential to add more value to their work compared with traditional approaches — although a substantial percentage believe a lack of knowledge or resources is their most significant obstacle to adopting agile.[4]

Suffice it to say, technology forms the critical backbone of effective Agile internal auditing. Employing technology to automate repetitive manual tasks frees auditors to perform more activities that create value for the business. Technology is also integral to effective collaboration and client involvement. Having a single source of truth for all risk and controls data promotes simplicity and eliminates inefficiencies inherent to a manual audit environment. Specifically, cloud-based platforms with automated notifications power timely insights and responses, more effective and frequent communication between internal audit and its clients, and greater visibility into project status for all stakeholders.

Data Analytics Help Auditors Know Their Business

Data analytics in the context of internal audit typically refers to technology that enables the testing of large data sets, allowing auditors to test full populations, identify anomalies, expand their risk coverage, and provide greater assurance. However, as internal audit faces increased pressure to develop more powerful and data-driven insights, analytics can now refer to a range of data analysis, automation, and business intelligence capabilities. I believe the future of data analytics lies in internal audit successfully harnessing those various capabilities to help organizations continuously monitor organizational risk and drive an integrated risk-first, data-centric approach to auditing. This empowers audit functions to provide real-time assurance, address key risks, and provide valuable insights to the business.

Success in today's data-first environment is nearly impossible without having a centralized system of record. Any effort to employ data analytics to drive assurance and quality insights is useless without reliable data. As PwC noted in a recent *State of the Internal Audit Profession* report: "Organizations cannot make the best use of emerging technologies without trustworthy data — meaning, data that is clean, accurate, and accessible."[5]

If your organization has not yet digitized its audit program, begin by unifying your audit, risk, and compliance data in a system of record that serves as the single source of truth and can integrate with data sources used by other departments. If your organization is already using a data analytics solution, look for an audit management solution that can integrate with it. Finally, it is important to recognize that maturing your business's data analytics capabilities is an ongoing process that often takes years. Approach the process incrementally and seek solutions that can integrate with other technologies your business employs so that they can grow with you.

Employing Emerging Technologies Is Crucial to Leading Change

In addition to audit automation platforms, innovative internal audit functions are increasingly leveraging emerging technologies. One example is automated controls testing, especially for control areas that are standardized, such as where tickets and fields are consistently used.

Robotics process automation: This automated controls technology entails the use of bots and software applications that can be programmed to perform basic human tasks that are typically rote or manual in nature. The main benefit of utilizing RPA in internal audit processes is that a bot can take care of repetitive manual tasks, freeing up time for auditors to perform more value-add activities. Areas where RPA can make the biggest impact in creating efficiencies for internal audit include:

- Data gathering and cleansing for analytics.
- Data gathering and classification for risk assessments (also inherent in audit automation software).
- Processing data populations during initial evidence gathering for controls.
- Internal audit project management areas (also inherent in audit automation software).

Artificial intelligence: AI simulates human decision-making and thinking by using sophisticated algorithms that learn based on transactions they are fed. These technology platforms can help internal auditors by automating important activities such as risk forecasting. For example, one application employs AI to analyze transactions in a general ledger and automatically organize them into groups of high, medium, and low risk. The benefits are that AI can be more comprehensive and effective than random sampling and can also flag anomalies and indicate where risks are likely at the transaction level.

Blockchain: A blockchain is a digital ledger created to capture transactions conducted among various parties in a network. According to a recent study sponsored by the American Institute of Certified Public Accountants (AICPA), blockchain technology offers an opportunity to streamline certain financial reporting and audit processes. I expect audit and assurance will evolve with blockchain, by necessity, as it is adopted by more industries. An example of how this might develop is the potential for supporting software to enable continuous auditing of blockchain transactions.[6]

Integrated Risk Management: The Key to Building Strong Relationships

While improving internal audit processes using automation software and emerging technologies is a noble and appealing goal, it is important to consider an integrated approach. Rather than simply thinking of how to improve audit lifecycle processes, forward-thinking internal auditors should consider how risk is managed across the entire organization.

The research and advisory firm Gartner defines integrated risk management (IRM) as "a set of practices and processes supported by a risk-aware culture and enabling technologies that improve decision-making and performance through an integrated view of how well an organization manages its unique set of risks." For the organization to understand the full scope of its risks, there should be a comprehensive view of risks across all business units and risk and compliance functions, as well as key business partners, suppliers, and outsourced entities.[7] An IRM approach is beneficial in reducing siloed risk domains and supports dynamic business decision-making via risk-data correlations and shared risk processes.

Developing this understanding fundamentally requires the collaboration of internal audit, risk, and security leaders, which is why a fully integrated approach to risk management is highly compatible with a combined assurance effort. Audit, risk, and compliance leaders who successfully deploy a cohesive IRM approach, supported by enabling technologies that can talk to one another via data integrations, can greatly expand risk coverage and empower their organizations to act on risks in real time.

Creating Time Is Creating Value

So why aren't more organizations joining companies such as UBSI in adopting promising new technologies? Part of the problem lies in the short-sighted view that both technology investment and internal audit generally are considered cost centers rather than value creators. Indeed, I have often lamented that internal audit is wrongly among the first to see cutbacks during economic downturns.

It is important that organizations recognize that technology investment in internal audit can be a capacity multiplier when done strategically, and internal auditors must be prepared to make the case on the return on technology investments. This is where having a change-agent mindset helps. We know the technology exists to make internal audit more effective and efficient, so we must be **bold enough** to advocate for the change and investment that create value.

Ultimately, internal audit leaders can make a compelling case by clearly articulating where an automation solution can save administrative hours in their audit workflows and identify where those saved hours would be redirected. Equating these resource hours to savings or increased productivity helps to build an even stronger case. After all, creating time is creating value.

How to Begin Building a Change-Enabling Foundation

One of the biggest takeaways from this chapter should be that having the right technology in place is foundational to enabling change that creates value. Internal auditors who are still performing their engagements manually should prioritize digitizing their audit program by unifying their audit, risk, and compliance data. A best practice is to seek a technology solution that:

- Enables remote collaboration with team members, stakeholders, and consultants and external auditors.
- Serves as the single source of truth for all audit, risk, and controls data.
- Has end-to-end automated workflows from planning to testing to reporting and issue management.
- Enables and empowers integrated risk management and combined assurance.

While various platforms offer differing features, the following are basic qualities that any leading technology solution should have:

Deep domain expertise. Whether it is Slack for instant messaging or Zoom for unified video communication, enterprises have found greater value from using software solutions that are purpose-built for specific departments, use cases, or industries, versus one-size-fits-all solutions. The marketplace now provides a wide variety of ideal options that address the nuanced needs of individual teams and can integrate with other solutions.

Bottom-up product development. User experience is key. Best-in-class solutions today employ a "bottom-up" product development approach focused on use cases specific to the department and are consequently optimized for the end users. This approach positions all members of an organization or team to successfully use the product. The software industry has seen that products with the best user experience typically have the best adoption and engagement rates.

Intuitive user experience. Optimizing technology must also consider ease of use to extract valuable data and insights in real time. Best-in-class technology solutions are designed to automate manual processes, consolidate data into a core system of record, and be flexible enough to manipulate and configure data into key insights, reports, and dashboards that support high-impact business decisions. Although this is true across all enterprise software solutions, it is especially relevant for audit, risk, and compliance software, whose users are facing increasing pressure to deliver risk-first, data-driven insights to executive management for agile decision-making. This requires solutions that are intuitive for the user.

Optimized for collaboration. As enterprises become increasingly connected, the ability for various users across the business to collaborate in a platform has increased in importance. Cloud-based solutions that are built to integrate with other cloud technologies, including Microsoft 365, Slack, and Google Suite, are highly valuable because they enable users to work within the native platforms they prefer while maximizing the potential of department-specific software. Additionally, solutions that embrace connectivity and collaboration resonate much better with customers.

The COVID-19 pandemic that emerged in 2020 fundamentally altered how people work on a day-to-day basis, and it clearly demonstrated just how integral technology is to the survival of the modern business. While internal auditors may have been slowly moving toward more integrated platforms prior to the crisis, the rapid shift to a fully remote workforce highlights the need for technology that enables organizationwide collaboration and automates administrative activities. As our profession inexorably moves from manual to automated audit engagements, those who understand and embrace technology as an enabler of value creation will lead our profession as true agents of change.

CHAPTER 7
Agents of Change Aren't Secret Agents

— • • • • —

The greatest discovery of all time is that a person can change his future by merely changing his attitude.

— Oprah Winfrey —

Anyone who spends time with the best internal auditors will quickly discern that there is a quiet passion that drives them. It is built on a genuine desire to help their organizations, respect from those with whom they interact, and unwavering pride in the service they provide. These characteristics — passion, desire, earned respect, and pride — are in the DNA of internal audit change agents.

Yet, even among top performers in our field, many struggle to communicate what they do and how their work adds value for their organizations. This challenge is so commonplace in the profession that we've learned to joke about it. Take the one about the man who instructs his child to tell his classmates that he works at McDonald's, because it's easier than explaining he is an internal auditor.

This self-deprecating attitude is pervasive and can be counterproductive to achieving the status of change agents in the eyes of our stakeholders. The profession is damaged by just this kind of misguided humility and reticence, which I have seen time and again among my peers as I've traveled the world as president and CEO of The IIA.

In contrast, agents of change successfully graduate from simply telling their own story to reshaping how the profession is seen. They are excellent storytellers who can inspire confidence and build trust. Indeed, Spotify's Kenneth Chen identified the ability to be influential and effectively communicate as the top skill he looks for when hiring managers for his audit function.

Recasting the Internal Audit Story

To formulate internal audit's story, we can begin with a gap analysis: Identify where we are and where we want to be in the eyes of our stakeholders and the general public. However, accurately identifying how internal audit is currently perceived can be tricky. There are many variables that influence the view, including differences in industry, organization size, complexity, and maturity; the level of regulation, compliance, and competition; the portfolio of risks most relevant to each organization; vulnerability to disruptive innovation; and the economic model under which organizations operate.

The easier part of the gap analysis is to identify where we want to be. So, let us begin there. Imagine a scenario in which internal audit's value to organizations is clearly and commonly understood. This is not as hard as one might think, mostly because a lot of the thinking has already been done for us. As I noted earlier in the book, The IIA's 2030 vision statement helps crystalize where we want to be as a profession: *Internal audit professionals are universally recognized as indispensable to effective governance, risk management, and control.*

That serves as a sound starting point. But I would argue that we need to take the vision one step further. Not only should the profession be recognized as indispensable to effective governance, risk management, and control, it also should be recognized as an indispensable element of value creation within the organization. So, we have set a lofty goal; now let's see how close we are to achieving it.

Is Indispensable Within Reach?

There is little debate that reliable assurance over the effectiveness of governance, risk management, and control adds value to an organization, and that a sufficiently resourced, independent internal audit function can deliver it. To be sure, as risk challenges become more complex and the speed of risk accelerates, stakeholders are increasingly attuned to the value of assurance. Therefore, identifying where stakeholders turn for assurance provides part of the answer to whether internal audit is considered indispensable.

One of The IIA's signature annual reports, *OnRisk*, is an excellent resource to gauge how we are doing on this front. For those unfamiliar, *OnRisk* provides a unique and highly valuable examination of risk as viewed by internal audit *and* its stakeholders. Through qualitative and quantitative surveys, it examines the perspectives of the board, C-suite, and internal audit on key risks. While the greatest value *OnRisk* brings is to illuminate the status of alignment among key risk management players, it also gives us a glimpse into where internal audit fits into the risk management process in the eyes of our stakeholders. The survey for *OnRisk 2021: A Guide to Understanding, Aligning, and Optimizing Risk* asked where organizations turn to for assurance. The results were decidedly mixed.

Exhibit 7-1: Assurance Conversation

On average, CAEs provide assurance on 4 or 5 of the risks listed below — most commonly cybersecurity, third party, business continuity/crisis management, and data governance.

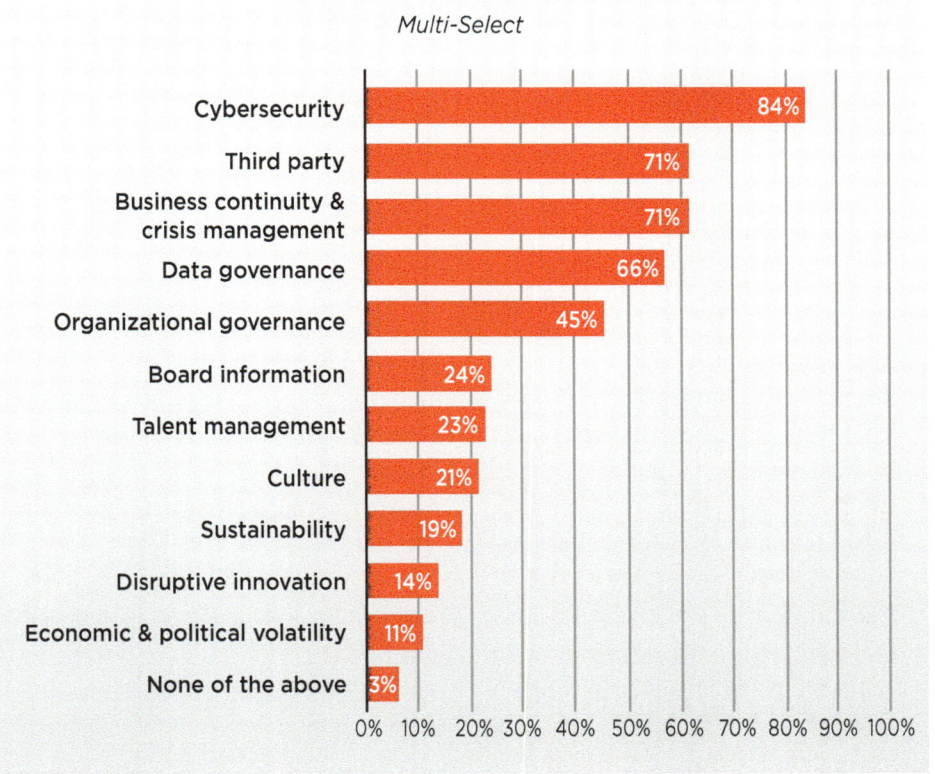

Q7. Which of the following risks do you provide or anticipate providing assurance on in 2020 and/or 2021?

Multi-Select

Risk	Percentage
Cybersecurity	84%
Third party	71%
Business continuity & crisis management	71%
Data governance	66%
Organizational governance	45%
Board information	24%
Talent management	23%
Culture	21%
Sustainability	19%
Disruptive innovation	14%
Economic & political volatility	11%
None of the above	3%

While a significant majority of CAEs said they provide or anticipate providing assurance over cybersecurity, third-party risks, business continuity and crisis management, and data governance, their attention to other key risks quickly fell off, as shown in **exhibit 7-1**.[1]

Exhibit 7-2: Organizational Relevance

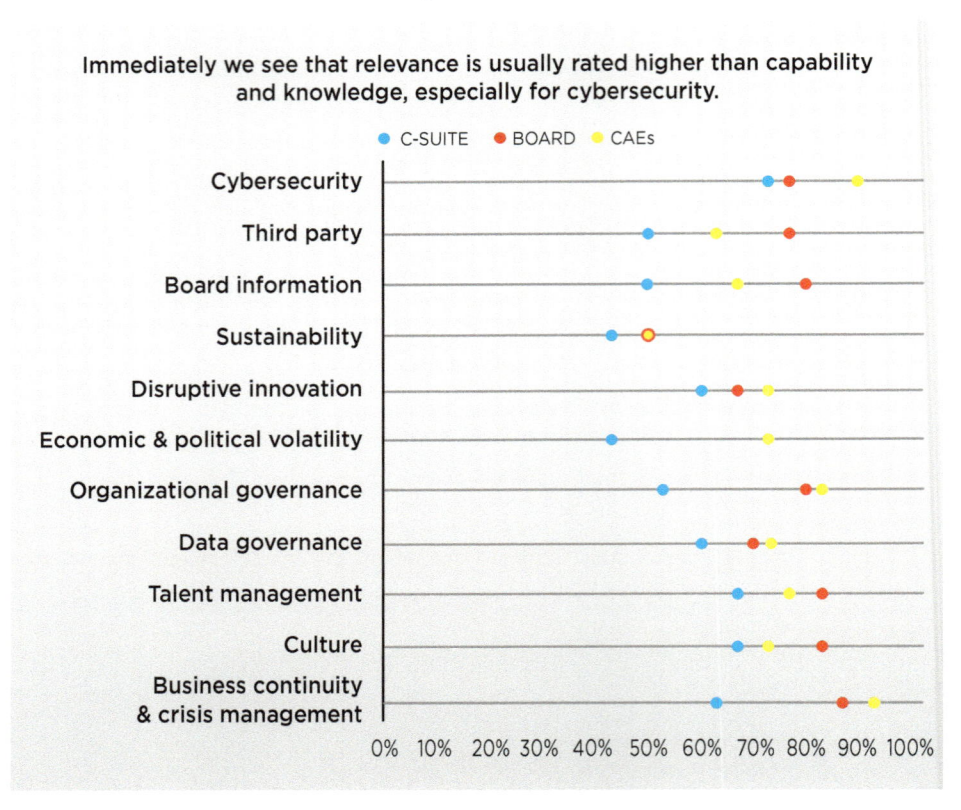

Immediately we see that relevance is usually rated higher than capability and knowledge, especially for cybersecurity.

● C-SUITE ● BOARD ● CAEs

Cybersecurity	
Third party	
Board information	
Sustainability	
Disruptive innovation	
Economic & political volatility	
Organizational governance	
Data governance	
Talent management	
Culture	
Business continuity & crisis management	

But when we compared the levels of assurance to those risks that the C-suite and boards identified as most relevant, internal audit was off the mark. C-suite and board respondents ranked talent management and culture as the second- and third-most relevant risks, while fewer than a quarter of CAEs reported providing assurance in these two areas, as illustrated in **exhibit 7-2**.[2]

The significance of this gap is twofold: Not only is internal audit providing minimal assurance in two risk areas ranked highly by its key stakeholders, but the data suggest that, as a result, stakeholders are turning elsewhere for that assurance. If internal audit is to be viewed as indispensable to governance, risk management, and control, it must be the primary source of assurance on *all* key risk areas.

OnRisk 2021 offers additional insight into internal audit not being viewed as indispensable to assurance.

From the report:

> "Data from both qualitative and quantitative . . . surveys suggest that truly independent assurance is often lacking, and the sources of assurance are typically inconsistent. Leaders generally feel the level of assurance they are getting is satisfactory, regardless of where it comes from. However, this *laissez-faire* approach fails to address the value of an independent assurance assessment."[3]

Leaders believe the processes and procedures surrounding assurance could improve in execution and impact, according to the report. However, *OnRisk* uncovered inconsistencies in the maturity of assurance among organizations, with one manufacturing C-suite executive commenting, "Our processes and procedures are old-fashioned. We just tick the box, make sure we have something with assurance. It's more mechanical, not as relevant and not evolved as much as it should be."[4]

The role and perception of internal audit within the organization also affects the quality of assurance, with one retail board member observing, "I've seen a big difference in companies in terms of the role of (internal audit). In some cases, they're a policeman, people don't really like them. In other cases, they're a real business partner to improve controls and seen as a resource for well-trained employees."[5]

Finally, the level of trust in internal audit, how internal audit leaders are viewed, and the culture of the organization also play significant roles. The same retail board member noted, "It depends on the culture of the organization, and the person leading [CAE] is so important. . . . If the organization doesn't embrace the department and it's not an integral part of the business . . . you have to be independent but have good relationships."[6]

OnRisk findings suggest not only that internal audit is not yet indispensable, but that assurance is not synonymous with internal audit and our stakeholders do not typically distinguish between assurance and *independent* assurance. We can conclude that our goal of being "universally recognized as indispensable" is greatly influenced by our reputation, the level of stakeholder trust, and how we promote the value of independent assurance. So, it is here where we must focus on telling our story.

Forging an Effective Communication Strategy

Managing reputations and earning trust are significant challenges. The first step to forging an effective communication strategy is to have better understanding of both.

Telling people what we do and convincing them of its value would seem to be a simple and straightforward task. After all, we carry out our jobs daily and know each step in our audit engagements. However, knowing our profession and effectively communicating how it helps the organization achieve its goals are vastly different things. What's more, as Spotify's Kenneth Chen noted, the challenge is more than just telling people about internal audit, it's about "selling" them on the value of internal audit.

There are any number of ways to look at reputation, but for our purposes here, a simple dictionary definition will suffice: Reputation is a widespread belief that someone or something has a particular habit or characteristic. Influencing any widespread belief is a complex endeavor that requires not just setting a clear and concise message — *internal audit is indispensable to good governance, risk management, and control* — but also persuading the audience of that message's validity, relevance, and accuracy.

The Principles of Persuasion[7] offered by Influence at Work provides some intriguing insights into how to influence what others think, which is ultimately what we want to accomplish with an effective communication strategy. Influence at Work breaks down the art of persuasion into six key principles: reciprocity, authority, consistency, liking, consensus, and scarcity. By applying the six principles to internal audit, we can begin forging our strategy.

Reciprocity. **Be the first to give, and make sure it is personal and unexpected.**

This principle taps into the positive feelings created when someone receives a pleasant surprise. Internal audit practitioners can accomplish this by telling clients not just what's wrong but also what's right.

Authority. **People follow the lead of credible, knowledgeable experts.**

Keeping stakeholders informed of the internal audit team's credentials and certifications builds its reputation as a source of expertise. Even something as simple as mentioning an audit team's years of experience or number of IIA certifications during introductory meetings can help build authority.

Consistency. **Looking for small but voluntary, active, and public commitments can lead to greater commitments.**

This can apply to getting clients to openly agree to adopt easily implemented audit recommendations, such as posting in the breakroom a list of tips on how to avoid and report phishing emails. This will make it easier to accept recommendations in the future for weightier actions, such as implementing formal anti-phishing training.

Liking. **People are more likely to like things that are viewed as similar, complimentary, and cooperative.**

Building relationships with clients outside of formal engagements helps put a familiar face on internal audit. Assigning specific teams or managers to work exclusively with certain departments can help build rapport and likeability without sacrificing independence or objectivity.

Consensus. **People look to the actions of others to determine their own.**

Liking can help build consensus. As more audit clients learn to appreciate and collaborate with internal audit, others will follow suit.

Scarcity. **People want more of those things they can have less of. Communicate the unique benefit and what they stand to lose.**

This principle requires an existing awareness of internal audit's value. In some organizations, less internal audit would be viewed as a positive! However, once internal audit builds authority and consensus, and demonstrates its value, communicating the consequences should internal audit be cut will be easier.

Formally Updating Our Story

A leading practice that I have promoted to CAEs for many years is to periodically produce a report on internal audit's performance and accomplishments. Such periodic disclosures were mandated when I was a U.S. government inspector general. But generating such reports is also widely practiced in the private sector. Whether produced annually or more frequently, these reports reaffirm to our stakeholders the value we are delivering for the organization.

One of the world's most respected companies, Coca-Cola, uses an annual Stewardship Report prepared by the corporate audit department to update stakeholders. Barry Ballow, CAE at Coca-Cola, said he incorporates four pillars into his annual report: quality, people, capability, and productivity/innovation. Here's how he does it.

Quality. This part of the report identifies the improvements the department made during the past year, particularly as they applied to IIA *Standards* quality assurance self-assessments. It also includes stakeholder feedback. In short, it communicates how and why internal audit is doing a good job.

People. This updates stakeholders on certifications earned, new hires, and promotions. It includes assessment of staff by those outside of internal audit as well, such as an engagement survey within the company.

Capability. Here, the audit department tracks advancements in team capabilities and provides an update on its digital journey. For example, it includes details on the use of tools, such as process mining, new and different digital approaches, and improved access and use of data.

Productivity/innovation. Of particular focus is the section in Coca-Cola's Stewardship Report that addresses the internal audit function's effectiveness. It covers budget and headcount, and maps those measures against maintaining high quality and investing in digital capability. It addresses improvements in processes, such as Agile auditing; automation, such as the use of dashboards populated directly from data software; and the strategy of leveraging all department resources globally.

"It's a bit of a marketing tool, but it is important to market the value add," Ballow said. "People understand our role in governance, that we are a required function in a large, publicly traded company. What they don't see is how we are innovative, how we are driving improvements, and how we are not immune to different stresses that they are feeling."

By recognizing the tools and techniques available to influence reputation, then applying them to daily actions, processes, and reports, such as Coca-Cola's Stewardship Report, we can begin to forge a strategy on reputation.

As a federal inspector general, I had a statutory obligation to update my agency, Congress, and the public on the work of our organization semiannually. Those reports could have simply been a sparse and unassuming recounting of the number of audits and investigations we undertook during the preceding six months. But like many of my fellow IGs, I recognized the opportunity that the reports presented to "tell our story" as an office of inspector general (OIG). So our reports were well-produced, attractive chronologies of our progress in fostering efficiency, economy, and effectiveness within the agency. I also took the time to personally add to our story. I signed my last semiannual report as inspector general of the Tennessee Valley Authority (TVA), a federally owned corporation that provides power and other services to millions in the southeastern United States, in October 2001. In my cover letter, I wrote:

> "Consistent with our newly adopted strategic plan, we made significant progress during the period in aligning the organization to better support the needs of our stakeholders. In this regard, we reorganized our audit operations to provide better emphasis on the core business processes of TVA, including energy operations. In addition, we created a separate team to provide advisory services to TVA officials and members of Congress with questions about TVA operations. We also realigned our investigative resources to facilitate our role in ensuring integrity in TVA operations.
>
> "We have featured the United States flag on the cover of this report as a reflection of our sympathy and solidarity with those directly affected by the tragic events beginning with the September 11, 2001, terrorist attacks on America. We stand ready to assist fellow law enforcement agencies in any way possible during this time of national crisis."[8]

The report went on to highlight the work of the OIG during the period, and included insight into our strategic planning process, highlights of audits and investigations undertaken, and honors and accolades bestowed on the TVA OIG by other federal organizations. Our objective in producing the report was to create awareness about our effectiveness in executing our statutory oversight mission, and to inspire confidence in our key stakeholders.[9] We were — simply — telling our story.

Communication and Marketing

A facet that complicates internal audit's struggles with improving its reputation is that many in the profession see any attempt to promote or communicate our value as unseemly. There has always been an aversion among internal auditors to come off as used-car salesmen. Yet, we see examples of two top companies, Spotify and Coca-Cola, where effective marketing of internal audit has led to greater success. In fact, I do not consider such initiatives to be "marketing" at all. Instead, I view it as awareness creation — a vital responsibility if we are to ensure our stakeholders understand our mission and potential in serving our organizations.

Every internal audit function can and should embrace techniques and practices to create awareness about its value and reputation, including:

- Holding one-on-one conversations with stakeholders — both formally and informally — where internal audit can solicit feedback.
- Developing professional presentations about the internal audit department through brochures, PowerPoint presentations, or intranet sites.
- Periodic reports on internal audit accomplishments, strategies, clarifications, and announcements, such as Coca-Cola's Stewardship Report.

But an even more fundamental practice is to educate internal audit practitioners to speak clearly and proudly about what we do. We should know instinctively what distinguishes us as a profession and be ready to declare it proudly. It is in that spirit that I offer a list of key messages to use if someone asked on an elevator, "What is it you do?"

- "I am an internal auditor!" This first line should be pretty self-explanatory. We should be proud and confident about being internal auditors. Few professions offer the opportunities to contribute to the success of our organizations like internal auditing does.
- "I serve my organization to protect and enhance its value." We're not just here to guard the doors and make sure people don't walk off with the assets. We're not just here to make sure others are not breaking the rules. We're here to make sure the organization achieves its objectives and creates value for shareholders/stakeholders.
- "I model integrity, objectivity, confidentiality, and competency every day." These are taken from the four elements of The IIA's Code of

Ethics. This is what we stand for as a profession, and it is something every practitioner should exhibit with every engagement and interaction.

- "I improve risk management, internal controls, and governance in my organization." This is at the heart of the definition of internal auditing articulated in the International Professional Practices Framework (IPPF). The definition speaks to adding value and improving an organization's operations. Simply, we make our organizations better.

- "I follow The IIA's *Standards* when providing assurance and advice." All professions have to have standards. They are what set individuals apart as professionals. That is why we must follow the *Standards*, to ensure the quality is there. I also urge internal auditors who have earned IIA certifications to proudly speak out. One should not be shy about proclaiming, "I am certified by The IIA to demonstrate the proficiency I have for carrying out my responsibilities as a professional internal auditor." As noted earlier in the chapter, authority is one of the principles of persuasion.

- "I am respected and admired because I am a guardian of trust!" This is a wonderful claim for any professional to make. Every internal auditor may not be respected and admired as a guardian of trust, but that should be their aspiration.

Those six simple messages shouldn't be viewed as a creed to be recited every time we're asked what we do. Instead, they should be used to add a little color to our description of internal auditing. They reveal an inspired and impassioned profession that is committed to making organizations better. We should be proud of what we do, and we should communicate that every day.

This brings us to one of the most difficult challenges in improving internal audit's reputation. Often, we can be our own worst enemy.

The Humble Internal Auditor

Part of the indoctrination into all cultures is the fundamental concept of acceptable behavior or social norms. One that is present in nearly all cultures is the concept of collaboration. From a young age, we are taught that we can accomplish more through cooperation and partnership. In short, we are told to "play well with others." Implicit in that social norm is the concept of humility. Simply, humility is having or showing a modest or low estimate of one's own importance and that, in order to "play well with others," we must check our egos at the door.

But humility can be deceivingly complex. Nihar Chhaya, a corporate executive coach who has advised senior leaders at many global companies, addressed humility in leadership in a recent *Forbes* magazine article, offering a concise and insightful definition. Humility is not about avoiding recognition of our strengths.

> In other words, being humble is not about putting yourself down; it's about recognizing that, despite your strengths and weaknesses, accomplishments, and mistakes, you don't deserve any different treatment than anyone else.[10]

Chhaya bases his definition in part on the views of German entrepreneur Karl Albrecht, who sees humility as achieving emotional neutrality and overcoming a natural "competitive reflex." A closer examination of Albrecht's discussion on humility provides additional insight into what humility "is not."

Consonant with the premise of what humility is not, as I think of it:

> It's not letting others "push you around."
>
> It's not being a doormat, a sucker, or letting people "walk all over you."
>
> It's not constantly sacrificing your interests to those of others (and then feeling like a victim or a martyr).
>
> It's not avoiding conflict or confrontation — not of your making, anyway — for the sake of "being nice."
>
> It's not about hiding your feelings or suppressing your views to avoid alienating others.[11]

Ironically, Albrecht's treatment of the topic actually makes the case that humility is underrated and misunderstood. He blames that partly on a "popular-media culture (that) is saturated with themes of conflict, combat, and conquest. Popular films feature cops chasing crooks; the military fighting terrorists; the lone avenger pursuing the evil-doers. We say we love peace makers, but our heroes are warriors. As a society, we like our celebrities to be cheeky, self-important, and even a bit narcissistic."[12]

He goes on to say that our society categorizes those who are genuinely humble as a bit strange. From an internal audit perspective, outsiders may indeed see us as a bit strange, or at least existing apart from the mainstream workforce. We are largely to blame for this misperception. We wrap ourselves in the flags of independence and objectivity, shield ourselves from the rest of the organization, and think of this as a virtue. Instead, it can be a straitjacket that limits our ability to elevate the profession in the eyes of our stakeholders.

As Coca-Cola's Ballow notes, "Humility and all of that is great, but we are in a business. It's important that we communicate our value to the business."

You can't raise awareness if you are unwilling to speak up about your accomplishments. You can't rise above the din of a host of others clamoring to be heard if you don't "toot your own horn." You can't expect busy stakeholders to seek out or single out your service and counsel if you don't even show up on their radar. In short, you can't be a change agent if you're a secret agent.

Promoting and Provoking Change

I have made the case that telling our story must include a sound strategy that raises awareness and appreciation for the value of independent assurance and builds trust among our stakeholders about our skills as individual practitioners. An important subtext to this strategy is not just understanding but embracing the concept that effectively telling our story is not boastful, arrogant, or inappropriate. Indeed, being an effective promoter of internal audit should be a part of every practitioner's DNA.

By raising awareness and building trust, we set the foundation for stakeholders to recognize the unique and informed perspective of internal audit. Implicit in this willingness to promote the profession must be a commitment to deliver outstanding service.

In *Trusted Advisors*, I explored the key attributes of practitioners who have achieved the title status. At the end of the book, I shared a list of definitions of trusted advisors offered by top internal audit leaders around the world. Those definitions capture key elements of high-performing practitioners.

> When it comes to outstanding internal auditors, the difference is not a matter of what but how. It is not that they do entirely different things; it's that they perform these practices in an outstanding way.

And along the way, they earn trust. They listen to others, they keep their self-interest under control, they display empathy, they share credit, they build relationships, they seek more complete solutions, and they focus on supporting the business. They have their eyes on the future and their feet in the present. Most of all, they cherish and protect the trust they earn, because they are well aware how quickly it can be lost.[13]

Agents of change take this concept one step further. They are the top performers, the *trusted advisors*, who recognize they can promote and foster change within their organizations. Agents of change understand that change begets change, and they are comfortable articulating how they can foster change. They build a culture of change by continually pushing to innovate. And they are never satisfied with the status quo.

PART THREE

THE RIGHT STUFF

CHAPTER 8
Business Acumen

— • • • • —

Either you're an agent of change or destined to become a victim of change. You simply can't survive over the long term if you insist on standing still.

— Norm Brodsky —

The overarching theme of this book revolves around change. In part one, I focused on how the internal audit profession came to be, how it has evolved over its storied history, and why radical transformation is imperative for the profession in today's volatile risk environment. Part two offered a frank assessment on the dire need to shift our attitudes and approaches in the key areas of process, agility, technology, and communications. In this final part, I address the individual practitioner and what is required to increase the ranks of agents of change within our profession.

In *Trusted Advisors,* I wrote extensively about the attributes it takes for internal auditors to become genuine "trusted advisors" within their organizations. I believe becoming a trusted advisor is critical to ultimately becoming an agent of change. As internal audit practitioners advance through their careers, they must see their journey as an evolution of skills, a consistent series of successes in executing on those skills, and building a reputation for excellence that elevates them in the eyes of key stakeholders.

That requires practitioners to not just possess deep knowledge and know how to communicate it, but also have the wherewithal to facilitate change on the basis of that knowledge. I've referred to this as having "The Right Stuff," borrowing the phrase from the 1979 Tom Wolfe book of the same name. The book was an homage to test pilots engaged in U.S. postwar research with experimental aircraft. It was from the ranks of those pilots that the first Project Mercury astronauts were selected for the NASA space program. While few internal auditors will have the opportunity to shriek beyond the speed of sound or venture into outer space, there are parallels between those daring test pilots and internal auditors who have the courage and willingness to take on the unknown to advance the profession and, more importantly, improve their organizations.

As I noted, understanding the *how* in addition to the *what* is vital, which I addressed in the introduction to *Trusted Advisors*:

> I believe that becoming a trusted advisor involves not just what you know (risk, control, and governance expertise) but also how you get things done (relationship acumen). Both are valuable attributes for internal auditors to possess, but it is only through their combination that one can truly become a trusted advisor.
>
> I've witnessed two internal auditors perform similar actions with very different outcomes. I suspect the reason is that the less effective internal auditor is strong in one trait and deficient in the other. Perhaps he has a strong technical background in internal auditing but can't communicate in a way that resonates with others. In fact, he may just be painful to work with. Or maybe he is a delightful lunch companion — humorous, charming, talkative — but with very little of substance to say. Excellence requires a balance of technical and soft skills.
>
> Internal auditors who rise above challenges and obstacles have achieved that balance by building a broad portfolio of complementary traits and attributes. These select few are not infallible — no one is perfect — but most do find success, and when they don't, they learn from their mistakes, avoid repeating them, and move on.

Trusted Advisors goes on to examine nine of the most desirable attributes of outstanding auditors based on a survey of members of The IIA's Audit Executive Center (AEC). Those traits are ethical resilience, results-focused, intellectual curiosity, open mindedness, dynamic communication, insightful relationships, inspirational leadership, critical thinking, and technical expertise. A similar global survey of internal audit leaders for *Agents of Change* found considerable overlap in key attributes. Indeed, the top attribute identified in the survey for this book — business acumen — is a powerful combination of many of the attributes I explored in *Trusted Advisors* (see **exhibit 8-1**).

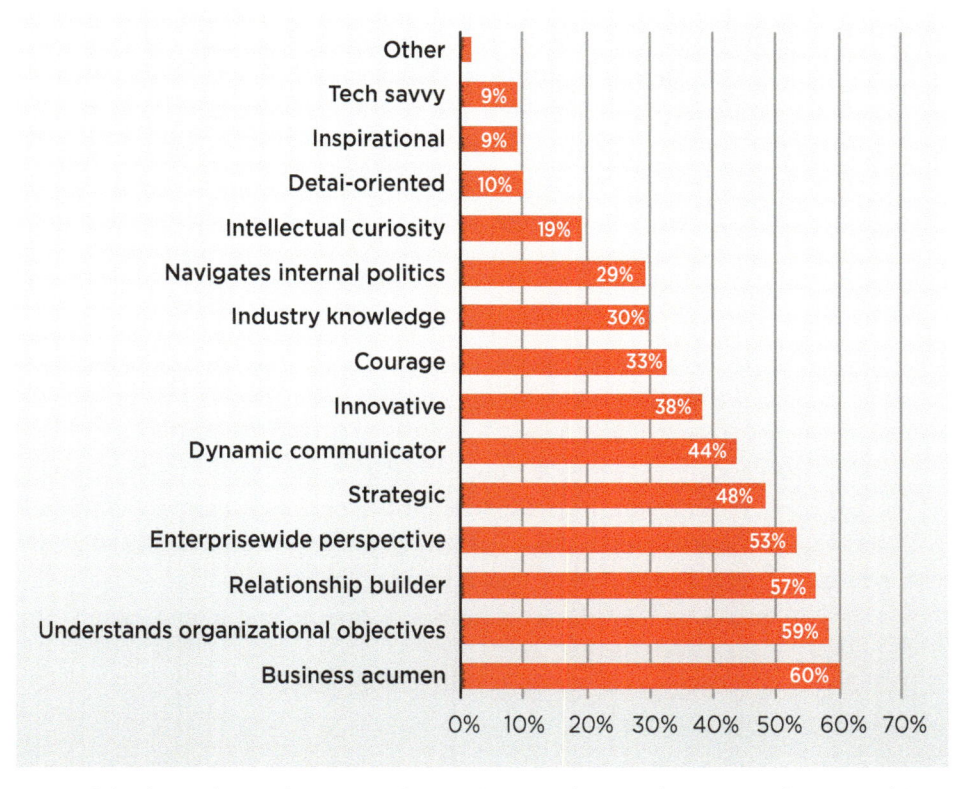

Exhibit 8-1: Key Attributes of Change Agents

Attribute	Percentage
Other	
Tech savvy	9%
Inspirational	9%
Detai-oriented	10%
Intellectual curiosity	19%
Navigates internal politics	29%
Industry knowledge	30%
Courage	33%
Innovative	38%
Dynamic communicator	44%
Strategic	48%
Enterprisewide perspective	53%
Relationship builder	57%
Understands organizational objectives	59%
Business acumen	60%

Note: Q10: What are the most important attributes an internal auditor must demonstrate to be a successful Agent of Change? n = 606

Candidly, possessing business acumen is fundamental for anyone aspiring to reach the highest levels of any profession, including internal auditing. Over my long career, I have seen how the elements of business acumen shape the success of internal auditors and how weaknesses in this area have held back others. I addressed business acumen briefly in *Trusted Advisors,* and that discussion provides a good foundation for understanding this attribute. This excerpt focuses on the value of strong business acumen and why it should be understood both generally (at the macro level) and at the enterprise level. Both are essential to being a true agent of change.

Generally speaking, individuals who possess business acumen are perceived to consistently exercise sound judgment and make decisions that result in favorable outcomes. They can assimilate information from an array of sources and use that new knowledge to propose sound strategic alternatives to address issues and problems. They also are always looking ahead trying to foresee opportunities and threats, the better to develop strategies to remain one step ahead of the competition. Possibly most important, they have the ability to see across the many areas of expertise within a company, such as finance, research and development, marketing, and IT; understand how decisions affect each of these areas; and work toward coordinating efforts to ensure shared success. This trait is called "breadth of understanding,"[1] and it was called out specifically in the AEC survey responses as a skill that can be achieved only by conscious effort and one that must be "continuously worked on."

A more succinct definition of business acumen is "keenness and quickness in understanding and dealing with a business situation in a manner that is likely to lead to a good outcome."[2] That definition packs a great deal of subtle meaning and demands into a mere 23 words. It requires *keenness, quickness,* and *understanding*. Therefore, for someone to display business acumen, they must be willing and eager to quickly learn enough about business to not only comprehend and grasp the subject, but to do so in a way that is likely to lead to a good outcome. That final requirement identifies a level of knowledge, insight, and sophistication that improves the chances of success.

General Business Acumen

Much has been written on business acumen. There are extensive descriptions as to what it constitutes. But in the end, I believe there are five elements critical to the fundamental process of how all organizations operate. Generally, they address finances, marketplace, operations, technology, and strategy. I believe that a keen understanding about each of these areas constitutes business acumen.

1. **Financial acumen.** This involves the metrics of business performance used to gauge success. It includes understanding and interpreting income statements, balance sheets, cash flow reports, forecasting and modeling, and other tools and techniques to track the financial health of the organization.

2. **Marketplace acumen.** This encompasses knowledge and understanding of competition, market drivers, consumer needs, marketing, disruptive innovation, and other influences on business success. It is critical to defining, creating, projecting, and protecting brand and reputation.

3. **Operational acumen.** This requires understanding factors that influence day-to-day operations and production, including the supply chain, third-party relationships, quality assurance, process improvement, and other systems that make the business run.

4. **Technology acumen.** This is the newest entrant to the components of business acumen, but it will likely grow quickly in importance. As we advance inexorably into the digital age, understanding how to leverage technology will be fundamental to the success of every organization. What's more, possessing technology skillsets — for example, understanding basic software program coding — to support the other components of business acumen will soon be as familiar and expected as Excel or PowerPoint skills were 10 years ago.

5. **Strategic acumen.** Probably the most important aspect of business acumen is recognizing and understanding the systems that define and influence an organization's goals and direction. In concert, they define business strategy, which drives operations, finances, and marketing. These systems include risk management; decision-making; data gathering, analysis, and use; short- and long-term planning; talent management; organizational culture; and more. I will delve deeper into strategic acumen in the next chapter.[3, 4]

In chapter 3, we examined the list of skills identified in the change agent survey. This examination included grouping those skills into three categories — professional, personal, and relational. Many of the characteristics identified in the professional category apply to general business acumen. Indeed, four of the top five attributes of change agents speak directly to it — business acumen, understanding organizational objectives, enterprisewide perspectives, and strategic (see **exhibit 8-2**).

That suggests survey respondents put a premium on the building blocks of general business acumen as core competencies of internal auditors who make the

Exhibit 8-2: Skills Categories

Professional	Personal	Relational
Business acumen (1)	Innovative (7)	Relationship builder (3)
Understands organizational objectives (2)	Courage (8)	Navigates internal politics (10)
Enterprisewide perspective (4)	Intellectual curiosity (11)	Dynamic communicator (6)
Strategic (5)	Detail-oriented (12)	
Industry knowledge (9)	Inspirational (13)	
Tech savvy (14)		

best change agents. In other words, those internal auditors who wish to drive organizational change as a result of their work must be willing to identify and commit to a set of core competencies — and business acumen is chief among them. It goes without saying that people are not born with business acumen. It is a learned skill developed and honed over time, requiring lifelong learning and perseverance. For those who wish to develop or enhance their business acumen, there are several key steps that I would recommend.

Find a mentor. The idea of the student learning at the feet of the master is as old as time itself. In the modern context, having a career guide is critical to learning the finer points of a complex and unforgiving business world. The benefits of having a sounding board and a place where it's safe to be vulnerable and get career advice are substantial, according to leaders at the Wharton School of Management. "It's a relationship where one can let one's guard down, a place where one can get honest feedback, and a place, ideally, where one can get psychological and social support in handling stressful situations," according to Wharton Management Professor Katherine Klein.[5]

Studies consistently show that good mentoring programs benefit both mentors and mentees. Mentoring programs increase employee engagement, and those in such programs are more likely to be promoted. Indeed, they have been proven to increase promotions for mentors and mentees five to six times more than non-participating employees.[6]

However, not every organization has a mentoring program, and poorly designed programs can do more harm than good. For example, a study that examined the protégé perspective found general support for the notion that, on average, bad programs are stronger than good programs in predicting protégé outcomes. A second study looked at the mentor perspective and found mixed support for the prediction that, on average, bad is stronger than good.[7]

So, one shouldn't rely solely on formal mentoring programs. The modern employee-employer relationship tends to be temporary. Unlike the business world I joined as a young internal auditor, few expect to retire from a company with a gold watch and pension after 30 years. Building relationships with an experienced leader outside of formal programs is a valuable option.

Get comfortable with financial statements and strategies. As I mentioned earlier in this chapter, part of developing financial acumen is understanding how money works in business. Digging out the details of finances and strategies can be challenging, but there are several ways to glean the information:

- Publicly traded companies are generally required to report periodically on their organizational structure, equity holdings, subsidiaries, employee stock purchases and savings plans, legal proceedings, controls and procedures, material weaknesses, executive compensation, and more.
- Such reports are often accompanied by quarterly earnings calls, in which company executives address details on strategies and forecasts.
- Annual reports are common to publicly traded and privately held companies. These can provide a great deal of detail on organizational finances.
- Financial information on public-sector organizations — those that operate with public funds — also is readily available. Local, state/

provincial, or federal treasuries typically collect and make available a great deal of information on finances and expenditures.

Pay attention to business news. Business media invest substantial resources to learn and disseminate information about individual companies as well as general business and economic trends. Identifying and closely monitoring credible business news outlets for information is a good practice.

Read, read, read. Whether through quarterly earnings reports, books on business, or biographies on successful entrepreneurs, internal auditors who wish to develop and maintain a healthy business acumen must remain informed.

Commit to lifelong learning. Practitioners must dedicate themselves to not just building core competencies, such as business acumen, they also must nurture and strengthen those competencies once achieved.

Know Your Business

As I have shared frequently over the years, one of the most common complaints I hear from management about internal audit is "they don't know the business." In such cases, management sees internal auditors as book smart on internal controls and risk management, but not street smart on what makes the company run. To truly transcend the ceiling below which management thinks we live, we need to have a deep understanding of our own organizations — regardless of the sector.

Having cultivated strong general business acumen is simply not enough. You must also learn how to apply and leverage that competency within your organization if you have any hope of being an agent of change. Effectively applying business acumen within the parameters of your specific role in the organization while staying true to the definition, mission, *Standards*, and ethical guidelines of the profession will be challenging, but it can be done.

There are at least three additional competencies a change agent must cultivate: build lasting professional relationships, operate strategically, and become a relentless innovator. I will go into each of these areas in depth in the next three chapters, but we should first examine how they are supported by business acumen at the enterprise level.

Relationship Acumen

Over many years, I have written and spoken extensively about relationship acumen. I rate relationship acumen on par with business acumen as table stakes for becoming a change agent. As you can imagine, relationship acumen has been the topic of many conversations over my career in internal auditing. One of the most insightful was my discussion with Kevin Patton, director of internal audit for The Ohio State University, who is a staunch supporter of relationship building.

It was his emphasis on the importance of relationship acumen in higher education that sparked an epiphany in me about its role in the agent of change journey. What follows is a short excerpt from *Trusted Advisors* of my conversation with Patton.

> "In corporations, the decision-making process is very top-down. The CEO makes a decision, and it is disseminated down through the ranks. In higher education, we have a shared governance model. Faculty, administrators, even students have a say in how the university operates. So working together through relationships is paramount."
>
> Corporate executives who are brought into a university setting, Patton explains, often have trouble making the transition to this shared governance approach. "Shared governance depends on relationships — and, yes, building those relationships can slow down the process, but it is critical to getting needed buy-in."[8]

The final point Patton made offers a critical lesson for those who strive to become agents of change. Whether it is persuading others to share governance, share power, or simply earn their trust, learning to build and maintain relationships is critical.

Having solid business acumen supports the change agent's ability to communicate with stakeholders at their level. Understanding the fundamentals of the organization's finances, operations, marketplace, technology, and strategy combined with an enterprisewide perspective on risk, governance, and control place the change agent in a unique position to help the organization achieve its goals. However, if we cannot build relationships with key stakeholders, those skills and competencies are wasted.

Operating Strategically

Earlier in this chapter, I described strategic acumen as recognizing and understanding the systems that define and influence an organization's goals and direction. Those systems are intertwined and influence virtually all aspects of internal audit's work. Change agents not only understand risk management, but they also apply their knowledge of decision-making, short- and long-term planning, talent management, culture, and more to identifying areas where the organization can improve and excel.

Additionally, change agents recognize how those intertwined systems and relationships influence the actions of others within the organization. A critical part of operating strategically is recognizing how and when to take action, respond to challenges, and push for change. I explore the characteristics of the strategic internal auditor in more depth in chapter 9.

Relentless Innovation

To innovate is to make changes in something established, especially by introducing new methods, ideas, or products. This virtually defines the change agent mindset. While internal auditors are not expected to identify new product lines or introduce new technology to the organization, the change agent can leverage his or her business acumen and holistic view of the organization to see and promote such opportunities. Key to innovation is having the flexibility to think entrepreneurially and creatively as well as being willing to consider outside perspectives.

Put simply, internal auditors help the trains run on time. Change agents identify the need for and add new routes.

The Change Agent Value Proposition

Evolution and change must be consistent themes in the lives of change agents. It is logical to assume that the change agent value proposition is an evolution of the more traditional internal audit value proposition.

Some time ago, The IIA published a tool to help practitioners communicate the value of their work to primary stakeholders, including audit committees, boards of directors, management, and audit clients. Represented by three intersecting circles, the value proposition is based on the three core elements of value —

Exhibit 8-3: Value Proposition

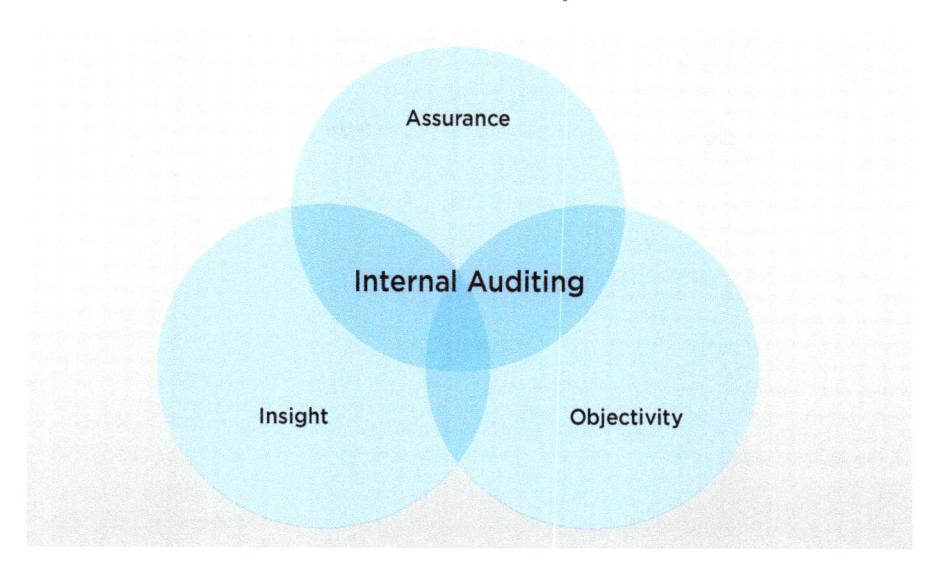

[Venn diagram with three overlapping circles labeled "Assurance," "Insight," and "Objectivity," with "Internal Auditing" in the center.]

assurance, insight, and objectivity — delivered by internal audit to an organization (see **exhibit 8-3**).

The 2015 update to the International Professional Practices Framework (IPPF) added a set of Core Principles for the Professional Practice of Internal Auditing. Among them is a requirement for internal audit to be "insightful, proactive, and future-focused." I view this as an important evolution of the insight component of the value proposition. Indeed, this leads me to add *foresight* to the internal audit value proposition.

Now that I've identified internal audit's value proposition as containing three distinct elements — assurance, insight and foresight, and objectivity – let's examine how agents of change can apply business acumen to each of those elements:

Assurance = Governance, Risk, and Control. Internal auditing provides assurance on the organization's governance, risk management, and control processes to help organizations achieve their strategic, operational, financial, and compliance objectives.

Insight and Foresight = Catalyst, Analysis, and Assessments. Internal auditing is a catalyst for improving an organization's efficiency by providing insight and advice based on analysis and assessment of data and business process. Foresight illuminates potential future threats, or risks, if critical actions are not taken, and is a critical — if not *the* critical — element of value. Successful organizations are able to navigate tomorrow's often rapidly emerging risks, not simply relive yesterday's.

Objectivity = Integrity, Accountability, and Independence. With commitment to integrity and accountability, internal auditing provides value to governing bodies and senior management as an objective source of advice enabled by internal audit's independence.[9]

Applying sound, fundamental internal auditing practices to help the organization achieve its strategic, operational, financial, and compliance objectives (assurance) is virtually synonymous with the benefits of general business acumen. The key value internal audit adds is its objective and independent assessment. As agents of change, we must make certain that we possess the business acumen to not just understand the organization's needs but to consistently demonstrate to our stakeholders how our business acumen, working in concert with independent, objective assurance, adds value. This addresses two of the three elements of the value proposition.

The final piece — insight and foresight — opens the door to not only enhancing that value but also to driving change. If we examine two critical components of insight and foresight, it is easy to make the case for internal audit driving change. Insight includes internal audit acting as a *catalyst for improving an organization's efficiency and effectiveness*. Foresight adds the dimension of internal audit illuminating *potential future threats, or risks, if critical actions are not taken, and rewarding opportunities if crucial actions are taken*. It is not a far stretch to conclude that internal audit can be *a catalyst for not only avoiding threats but also for pursuing opportunities*. That describes the agent of change value proposition.

In the past, I used a 2-by-2 matrix to illustrate the essential qualifications of a trusted advisor.

Exhibit 8-4 shows that being a trusted advisor is a function of at least two broadly framed capabilities that CAEs must possess: 1) risk, control, and governance expertise, and 2) strong relationship acumen.

It's time that I update that matrix to reflect the added components that lead to becoming an agent of change (see **exhibit 8-5**).

Exhibit 8-4: Ascending to the Level of Trusted Advisor

	Relationship Acumen	
	A Good Lunch Partner	Trusted Advisor with a Seat at the Table
	Taking Up Space	A Well-Kept Secret

Risk, Control, & Governance Expertise

Exhibit 8-5: Ascending to the Level of Agent of Change

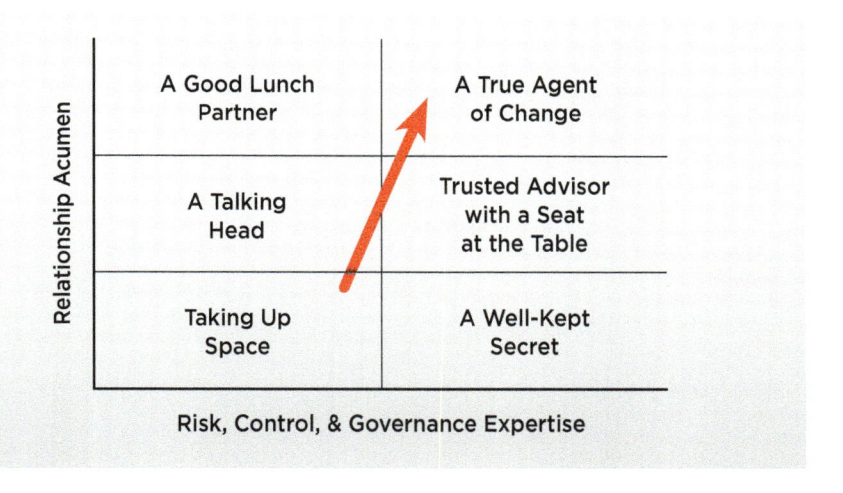

	Relationship Acumen	
	A Good Lunch Partner	A True Agent of Change
	A Talking Head	Trusted Advisor with a Seat at the Table
	Taking Up Space	A Well-Kept Secret

Risk, Control, & Governance Expertise

One of the simplest definitions of change is *to make or become different*. Agents of change do both by becoming something different as they grow from being trusted advisors and by making their organizations different and better.

CHAPTER 9
The Strategic Internal Auditor

*If you don't know where you are going,
any road will take you there.*

— Lewis Carroll —

As a young internal auditor, I concentrated all of my energies on learning the audit standards and how to deliver sound internal engagements that were well planned, conducted, and reported. I had no time for abstracts like "strategy." The word never even came up in my internal audit department. Eventually, I became a chief audit executive (CAE) and all of that changed. I began to understand why my predecessors had failed to win and sustain the support of internal audit's key stakeholders. They were focused on leading tactically sound internal audit functions, but they were never really focused more than a year ahead in leading the organization.

I began to contemplate what it would take for the internal audit function I had been selected to lead to deliver value and engender the support of stakeholders to make a greater investment in our department. I was formulating and executing a strategy without even realizing it. Then, almost three years after I was tapped to lead the internal audit department, something happened that fundamentally changed the way I saw the world. I was selected as one of only six civilians to attend the U.S. Army War College in Pennsylvania.

The name "War College" is a bit misleading. It is not an institution that teaches fighting wars or how to successfully deploy tactics in battle. On the contrary, the mission of the War College is "to educate and develop leaders for service at the strategic level." My year of residence at the institution helped equip me for a lifetime of serving subsequent roles with a strategic mindset. To any extent I ever became an "agent of change" in the organizations in which I later served, I attribute much of my success to the strategic mindset instilled in me at the U.S. Army War College.

While there, I learned to apply the principles of strategic thinking to how the Army was treating its internal audit resources. I wrote two or three papers that focused on the ramifications of downsizing the military's internal audit force, which I referenced in chapter 5. One of the papers was titled "Pay Now, and Pay Later." My message was simple: The Army was not being strategic by divesting itself of audit resources to address immediate budget reductions. Indeed, doing so eliminated the very tool it needed to identify cost reductions and savings opportunities necessitated by budget reductions. The situation was similar to that of a farmer who eats his seed corn to survive the winter. If you eat the seed corn, you will have nothing to plant later. It was the beginning of my infatuation with strategic thinking and internal audit.

The quote at the beginning of this chapter is a powerful one because it speaks a fundamental truth about strategy. *If you don't know where you are going, any road will take you there.* In other words, if there is no strategy, any solution will do.

Being Strategic Starts at Home

Before internal auditors can leverage a strategic mindset to be change agents within their organizations, they must be strategic in the way they drive change in internal audit itself. As a CAE, I have led every one of my audit departments through a strategic planning process almost immediately upon my appointment to the post. I view strategic plans like a roadmap, with a clearly marked destination (vision). Just as you should never embark on an extended road journey without a map, I believe you should never undertake leadership of an internal audit department without a strategic plan.

I have always taken a classical view of strategic planning, believing that a sound plan should chart a vision three to five years into the future. It also must clearly outline how the internal audit department will bridge the gap from the present state to an envisioned future state. Whether leading strategic plans of my own departments or advising CAEs who were undertaking their own planning efforts, I have subscribed to essentially the same strategic planning process:

- **Identify/validate internal audit's key stakeholders.** For a first-time effort at developing a strategic plan, it is essential to identify internal audit's stakeholders. This will typically include the board, management, and regulators (in some industries). During subsequent updates to the strategic plan, it is always advisable to revalidate the list of key stakeholders.

- **Articulate the needs and expectations of internal audit stakeholders.** Understanding the needs and expectations of internal audit's stakeholders is vital to ultimately determining the vision. This phase will typically include interviews and conversations with critical members of the stakeholder groups, when possible. It is also important to focus on the needs and expectations they have for internal audit in five years, not just in the present.

- **Undertake a SWOT analysis.** Brainstorming sessions with the strategic planning taskforce should be used to identify internal audit's strengths, weaknesses, opportunities, and threats. That can be helpful in an eventual gap analysis.

- **Identify critical assumptions about the future.** Focus on those external forces that are and are not controllable. Assumptions can include forecasts or trends, such as those that are economic, regulatory, environmental, or industry.

- **Forge a vision.** Once stakeholder needs, SWOT analysis, and critical assumptions are formulated, it is time to articulate the vision. The vision should be succinct and aspirational. At the conclusion of our strategic planning process at TVA's Office of Inspector General, we articulated a vision of "Illuminating today's challenges and tomorrow's opportunities." The vision should also align with the strategy of the enterprise. If your company is planning to expand globally in the next five years, your strategic plan should clearly align.

- **Undertake a gap analysis.** Once the vision is articulated, it's time to compare where you are with where you need to be. It is the gap analysis that enables the formulation of the goals and objectives that make up the heart of the strategic plan.

- **Articulate strategic goals.** Goals will guide the internal audit department in the ultimate achievement of the strategic vision. Strategic goals should articulate the desired outcome of the efforts that need to be undertaken. I have always preferred to limit the number of goals, and have focused on those things that have to be corrected/accomplished to bridge the gap and enable achievement of the strategic vision. For each strategic goal, there should be three to five objectives. An objective should be a measurable step needed to achieve the goal. I typically refresh objectives as progress is achieved toward a goal.

The process I have outlined is the one I prefer to use; you may prefer an alternative approach. But by all means, have a strategic plan. We will never be change agents in our organizations if we are not willing to commit to strategic change within the internal audit function itself.

Attributes of Strategic Internal Auditors

Strategic internal auditors are certainly capable of developing a strategic plan for internal audit. But not everyone who crafts a strategic plan is a strategic internal auditor. So, what does it take for an internal auditor to be truly strategic and be seen as strategic by management and the board? That was touched on in a recent edition of The IIA's *Global Perspectives and Insight*s series, "Elevating Internal Audit's Strategic Impact:"

> Internal audit is uniquely positioned to be a strategic partner. With reporting relationships to the chief executive officer (CEO) or other executive officer, audit committee, and the board, high-performing CAEs combine intelligence, expertise, diligence, and curiosity in a manner that positions internal audit for a critical strategic role. Despite this, CAEs are not generally recognized for the potential strategic impact that they can have on their organizations. For CAEs looking to elevate the strategic role of internal audit, several questions should be answered to take this next logical and desired step. Does the CAE understand the strategic mission of the organization at a deep level? Does the CAE understand the perspective of the CEO and board and make the effort to become a trusted partner, offering advice and solutions that address key problems? Is internal audit aligned with the strategic mission? Is internal audit anticipatory and proactive (rather than reactive)? Does the CAE provide assurance on risk management?[1]

As The IIA emphasizes, strategic internal auditors combine intelligence, expertise, diligence, and curiosity in exercising a strategic role in the organization. But is this the full inventory of characteristics that a strategic auditor must possess? A recent *Forbes* article by Paloma Cantero-Gomez on the critical skills of successful strategic thinkers offers even more insight into what it takes. I believe the list is particularly appropriate when assessing the strategic acumen of internal auditors:[2]

- **Vision.** According to Cantero-Gomez, "strategic thinkers are able to create and stick to a very clear visioning process." That is certainly true of internal auditors. As we discussed earlier, the ability to be visionary should begin with the vision for internal audit itself. Leaders in this profession have throughout its history been instrumental in crafting a future vision that enabled the profession to advance. Cantero-Gomez notes, "a clear, positive, and big enough vision is what inspires for action and pulls in ideas, people, and other resources." For internal auditors to be change agents, they must clearly grasp the vision of their enterprise, and bring their own strategic skills to bear on how change can facilitate achievement of the vision of the enterprise. They are not content to simply "count the beans," or even to advise on how the beans should be grown. Strategic internal auditors may well offer advice on whether beans are the right crop to grow.[3]

- **Framework.** Cantero-Gomez builds on the need for vision by pointing out that "vision should be carefully embedded within a framework. Successful strategic thinkers have the ability to define their objectives and develop an action plan with goals broken down into tasks specifically measured in terms of timeline and resources." This is where internal auditors can leverage their natural strengths in left-brain thinking (logic) with right-brain thinking (creative), which are integral to strategic visioning and action. Strategic thinkers are self-aware and, as Cantero-Gomez puts it, "they are conscious of their own biases and factor their own circumstances, perspectives, and points of view within this framework."[4]

- **Perceptiveness.** In its assessment of critical strategic thinking skills, Cantero-Gomez notes that "strategic thinkers are able to look around and understand the world from all different perspectives. They listen, hear, and read between the lines." This is a particularly important skill for the strategic internal auditor. Objectivity is a vital trait for our profession. If we undertake audits with preconceived biases, we do a disservice to those we audit and the enterprise as a whole. We complement that objectivity with keen perceptiveness and leverage creative thinking and intellectual curiosity in identifying causes and formulating solutions and future strategies. To be effective change agents, internal auditors must be keenly perceptive in identifying opportunities, not only for corrective measures, but for value creation through transformational change.[5]

- **Assertiveness.** Strategic internal auditors are confident enough in their skills and abilities to be assertive when needed in promoting change. As Cantero-Gomez notes, "after a comprehensive evaluation, (strategic thinkers) choose the way to go and walk firmly into it without vacillation. They may doubt, but they do not let the doubts fog the vision. They communicate effectively what they want and need by using clear orders while simultaneously respecting the thoughts and wishes of others." Internal auditors don't "give orders," but those who are trusted advisors certainly command attention when they offer recommendations and advice. Assertiveness in the strategic internal auditor is most frequently demonstrated by persistence. If at first the strategic auditor doesn't succeed, they try and try again.[6]

- **Flexibility.** One of the nine characteristics of outstanding internal auditors featured in *Trusted Advisors* was "open mindedness." I observed that "the truly outstanding internal auditors I have known thrive on change. They enthusiastically seek out opportunities to make quantum improvements in their approaches to audit and the solutions they identify when their audits identify risk management or control deficiencies."[7] Another word for the attribute I was describing is "flexibility," which happens to be one of the seven critical skills of strategic thinkers noted in the *Forbes* article. As Cantero-Gomez points out, "strategic thinkers are clearly aware of their weaknesses, so they are committed to seeking the advice of others. They are humble enough to be flexible and twist their ideas and framework as to truly achieve the desired vision. They do not confuse flexibility with lack of structure. They accept the rules of the game, because they are aware that, without rules, there is no fair game." Nothing could more aptly describe the open-minded internal auditor. Strategic internal auditors recognize that there are multiple paths to the same outcome and are more interested in the results that change will bring than in being right about how that change must be implemented.[8]

- **Emotional balance.** In the words of Cantero-Gomez, strategic internal auditors "are able to balance their emotions in a way that always favors the achievement of the ultimate goals." The finest internal auditors I have ever known have been even-keeled, and did not let their emotions impair their sound judgment. As Cantero-Gomez puts it, "whether they received positive or negative feedback, they [strategic thinkers] are able to deal with it, understand, and respond in a way that protects and progresses toward their desired outcome." It is the ability to contain emotions that often differentiates good internal auditors from those who are truly great at their craft. During my career, I have faced intense pushback from those whose areas of responsibility may have been criticized in my audits. But I learned from some of my earliest mentors in the profession that emotional responses to strong negative reactions from management rarely resolve disputes. Strategic internal auditors recognize that success is attained only if positive beneficial change results from their work. Acrimonious disputes with those whom they trying to persuade will most likely end in failure.[9]

- **Patience.** The seventh of the critical skills that strategic internal auditors must embrace is patience. As Cantero-Gomez notes, "strategic thinkers do not ignore that achievement is a long-term ride. Milestones all have a concrete time and moment. And success is the result of a process of strategically planned work and efforts. Strategic thinkers have the ability to be patient." Truer words could not be written about strategic internal auditors; they recognize that achievement of a vision is a long-term proposition. They also realize that change is the means by which strategic visions will ultimately be realized, and that patience will truly be a virtue if they are to be an agent of change. In the words of Leo Tolstoy: "The two most powerful warriors are patience and time."[10]

Avoiding the Pitfalls of Being a Tactical Internal Auditor

We are taught from the outset of our careers the importance of being (in the words of the internal audit definition) "systematic and disciplined." We become tactically focused on process that is often dictated by policies and procedures. We meticulously plan our engagements and document them in an audit program, which is often a step-by-step guide to undertaking the internal audit. We undertake the audit by gathering and tediously documenting the evidence necessary to draw conclusions. Finally, we prepare exhaustive reports that chronicle the results of our audits, which are then presented to those who are responsible for implementing corrective measures. We repeatedly undertake this process until many of us execute our roles with robotic precision. We become master tacticians in executing internal audits. Yet, to be agents of change, we must be anything but tactical. It is for this reason that the strategic internal auditor must avoid the pitfalls of being a tactician.

A few years ago, the Brainzooming Group published a short article highlighting six characteristics of strategic thinking skills as compared with tactical thinking. A review of this list highlights hurdles that classically trained internal auditors must overcome in their quest to be strategic internal auditors:

1. **A tactical thinker keeps opportunities and issues separate so that they are digestible.** The strategic internal auditor recognizes that the solution may not be to simply correct a problem. It may instead present an opportunity for the organization to take a completely different approach — one that will enhance value through greater efficiencies and effectiveness than could be achieved by simply correcting something that is broken.

2. **A tactical thinker looks at what is happening at face value.** A strategic internal auditor recognizes that the root cause may be far more complex than is evident on the surface. As I noted in *Trusted Advisors*: "Getting to the bottom of things requires more than just incessantly asking "why," as a child might do. If we did that, our clients would undoubtedly lose patience with us in short order, and our reputation for credibility would suffer." Strategic internal auditors do more than ask why. They exhibit strong critical thinking skills — "the ability to take information or a set of circumstances, consider the inherent challenges or weaknesses, identify deviation from acceptable criteria, and then do a root cause analysis to fully understand why something did or didn't happen."[11] That process often takes us to a very different conclusion than what might appear on the surface.

3. **A tactical thinker works to fill information holes, answering one question and moving to the next without asking any other questions in between.** The strategic internal auditor doesn't wait until an audit engagement is complete before applying critical thinking skills. They recognize that analyzing the results continuously may influence the next steps in evaluating a problem, and will likely yield more timely insights.

4. **A tactical thinker is focused on checking items off a list to get it finished.** A strategic internal auditor recognizes that, to reach the

strongest results, audit plans should remain dynamic. That kind of tactical thinking is a primary target of agile auditing, as discussed in chapter 5.

5. **A tactical thinker is sequential, focusing on one thing followed by another.** A strategic internal auditor recognizes that sequential thinking may limit their ability to observe the interconnected nature of systems and processes. It is only through a holistic examination of operations that transformational change can be envisioned and advised.

6. **A tactical thinker avoids complexity.** The strategic internal auditor embraces complexity, seeks solutions to challenges, and envisions opportunities to simplify complexity.[12]

It should be noted that tactical skills are still important when undertaking the internal audit mission. As Brainzooming notes, "The strongest businesspeople deliver on both strategy and tactics to create results."[13] However, strategic internal auditors recognize that tactical skills are simply enablers. They are important in undertaking the analysis that will ultimately enable the strategic mindset to formulate solutions that drive transformational change within the organization.

Strategic Internal Auditors and Transformational Change

Much has been written about transformational change. Simply defined, it is significant change designed to create "breakthrough value" for the organization. As Deloitte describes it, transformational change "involves strategic decisions that affect where you'll grow, how your organization operates, and what kinds of performance improvements you can expect."[14]

Given the profound nature of transformational change, is it reasonable to expect that internal auditors would be involved? I believe the answer must be an emphatic "yes!" While internal auditors certainly should not be the architects for such change, it is entirely reasonable to expect that they can be part of the process. If management and the board identify transformational change as a strategic goal of the enterprise, there will surely be risks and opportunities that should be identified and managed as part of the enterprise risk management system. Internal audit should ensure that associated risks are identified and included in its audit plan, as appropriate. More importantly, however, internal audit should be a strategic partner with management in seeking opportunities to drive transformational change.

Our contributions can come from insights on risks and controls and foresight on transformational opportunities. By leveraging the critical strategic thinking skills outlined in this chapter, internal auditors can leverage their seat at the table to be a strong advocate for change based on their knowledge of the business and their insights on the effectiveness of the organization's risk management, control, and governance processes.

Deloitte identified "six keys to unlocking breakthrough value in transformational change." I quote the opening section of each, and internal auditors would do well to remember and embrace them as they seek to be champions of transformational change:

1. **Begin with a strategy-informed ambition.** Leaders in business transformation typically have a clearly articulated, well-understood business strategy. Often an organization's strategic choices — although understood tacitly by senior leadership — are poorly translated into downstream implementation choices. The result? The dilution of value.

2. **Lead with capabilities.** Leaders in business transformation quickly focus and define the specific enterprise capabilities that will help achieve competitive advantage. In reality, only a small number of an organization's total capabilities play a critical role in helping the organization find new ways to differentiate and compete. Focusing on those critical capabilities can help deliver greater value, help leaders drive competitive advantage, and help the organization realize its business transformation ambition.

3. **Drive to value.** Leaders in business transformation articulate up front the value they expect to achieve through transformation, and they zealously monitor, measure, and track value throughout their transformation. Value should be the thread that links your business strategy and your transformation together. Take time to be explicit about exactly how you intend to create value. Then establish strong, clear connections to your execution plans.

4. **Build in sustainability.** Leaders in business transformation know that real value emerges over time through sustainable change that endures. To put the right capabilities, competencies, and change-adaptive culture in place for sustaining and growing the value of the transformation, data is essential. Leaders should use data-driven change

management solutions. Such solutions should support a quantifiable, analytical approach to managing attitudes, behaviors, and engagement. And they should be more than generic solutions that fail to address the unique challenges of the organization.

5. **Be agile and flexible.** Leaders today should be prepared to continuously evolve through transformation because the business and technology landscapes in which they operate are continuously evolving. Leaders should work hard to embed agility, innovation, and a disruptive mindset into every transformation initiative.

6. **Invest in program talent.** Leaders in business transformation recognize that the right leader and right talent will make or break the success of the transformation. A strong program leader should have influence and credibility within the organization to make major shifts and shape how work gets done. Assigning a respected and capable business leader is critical to establishing the credibility and importance of the transformation to the organization's strategic goals.[15]

Obviously, not all change that internal auditors influence in their organizations will be transformational change. In fact, virtually every audit or advisory engagement should result in some change — even if it is only corrective in nature. However, the more transformational the change, the more a strategic mindset will benefit the internal auditor. As we will explore in chapter 11, an innovative mindset will also be a valuable asset for the internal auditor who contributes to the organization's transformational change initiatives.

CHAPTER 10
On Being Relationship Centric

— • • • • —

Change before you have to.

— Jack Welch —

Persuading others requires a genuine level of trust. "You are just an internal auditor. Why should I listen to you when it comes to making a fundamental or critical change to my business?" Those we are trying to influence may not openly say that, but from my experience, it is certainly a barrier when we are trying to promote change. For that reason, it was not surprising to me that the CAE survey conducted for *Agents of Change* ranked relationship builder (66%) and dynamic communicator (44%) as the third and sixth most important attributes that an internal auditor must demonstrate to be an agent of change. Without those skills, we are stuck.

In chapter 8, I touched on how having solid business acumen supports the change agent's ability to communicate with stakeholders at their level. But that assumes a thorough understanding of the basic skills for relationship building in the workplace. Understanding how relationships are built and nurtured goes well beyond simply having a bubbly personality or an outgoing nature. I delve into that later in this chapter, but let's begin by addressing the benefits of building relationships.

There's significant research into the value of workplace relationships. Positive social interaction among co-workers is linked to mental and physical wellbeing. The opposite is true for social isolation. Researcher Elaine Houston, writing for *PositivePsychology.com*, explains this nicely:

"Psychologists have long identified the desire to feel connected to others as a basic human need, with interpersonal relationships having a significant impact on mental health, health behavior, physical health, and mortality risk (Umberson & Montez, 2010). Indeed, human physiological systems are highly responsive to positive social interactions."[1]

Houston's article goes on to cite research linking close relationships to protecting against the adverse effects of stress (Gable & Gosnell, 2011); social pain in the workplace to actual physical pain (Dunbar & Dunbar, 1998); cooperative, trusting, and fair workplace relationships triggering the brain's reward center (Geue, 2017); and positive social interactions boosting physiological resourcefulness (Heaphy & Dutton, 2008).[2]

Foundational skills for building strong relationships are well established, and for many, those skills are instinctive or commonsensical. However, others struggle even to achieve these basic skills without a focused effort. I won't dwell too long in this area because agents of change are assumed to have mastered the basics of relationship building, but I offer the following primer for those just beginning or early in their careers. The modified list below is taken from an article in *Indeed.com*, but they are commonly understood as the building blocks of positive relationships.

> **Verbal communication skills.** Verbal communication is essential to building strong relationships. Finding opportunities to contribute ideas and ask questions shows you are interested and open to hearing the ideas of others as well as motivated to contribute.
>
> **Nonverbal communication skills.** Nonverbal communication also can have an impact on how you build relationships with others. For instance, learning how to read body language can help you pick up on other people's emotions. Understanding and being conscious of your own body language and the signals you put out are just as important.
>
> **Listening skills.** Active listening is an essential part of communication. It includes making eye contact, being aware of nonverbal cues, and asking questions that show you are invested in the conversation. This not only shows that you respect the ideas of others, but it also indicates you care about all perspectives.

Networking skills. Meeting new people, exchanging ideas with other professionals, and offering assistance to other business professionals can help boost your networking skills. Effective networking skills increase professional reach and help form lasting professional relationships.

Team-building skills. Working as part of a team will almost always require effective relationship building. Develop your teamwork skills by practicing effective communication, showing respect for the ideas of others, and contributing and assisting where needed.

Empathy. Having empathy means you try to understand the feelings and emotions of others. Importantly, it involves experiencing another person's point of view, rather than just your own. Actively practicing empathy in the workplace signals to co-workers and managers your dedication to the overall success of the organization.

Emotional intelligence. Emotional intelligence combines several of the skills already discussed. It is the capacity to be aware of, control, and express one's emotions, and to handle interpersonal relationships judiciously and empathetically. Being emotionally intelligent means that you observe the dynamics in the workplace and find ways to contribute, help solve conflict, and generally work from a place of understanding.[3]

Before moving on, we should recognize that several of the basic skills outlined here are what I have been promoting for years in an internal audit context. Active listening and nonverbal communications should be part of the internal auditor's toolkit. Empathy and emotional intelligence also are vital in maintaining objectivity.

What's more, in *The Speed of Risk,* I address how to leverage basic relationship building to support continuous assessment of risk through a practice I call "shoe-leather assessments."

> "Another way to keep your risk assessment and audit plan up to date is what I like to call "risk assessment by walking around." This method is exactly as the phrase implies and relies on developing strong working relationships with key members of senior management. This way you know about new risks as soon as they do. Risk assessment by walking around may lack the discipline and structure of more formal assess-

ments, but it's a powerful strategy for keeping in touch with what's happening in your organization and may reveal new risks that your formal risk indicators do not. Given the number of business units and executives in large companies, risk assessment by walking around cannot be the responsibility of only the CAE; the entire internal audit department must be organized and deployed."[4]

Even once mastered, basic relationship building must be raised to an even higher level. We must elevate our affiliations beyond appreciation and trust to a level of admiration and respect. This is where our relationships with our stakeholders must end up if we are to become change agents.

In *Trusted Advisors*, I dedicated a chapter to insightful relationships and covered several facets of how internal auditors can elevate connections with stakeholders. That included a reference to research I did with the Korn/Ferry Institute to examine personal attributes that maximize the impact of CAEs. That research identified six key relationship-building skills typically demonstrated by outstanding internal auditors:

Positive intent. It is critical for the client to see the internal auditor as fair, independent, and objective in their approach and as someone who has everyone's best interests at heart. Trusted advisors demonstrate a positive intent that makes it clear they aren't set on being right — but on finding the right answer.

Diplomacy. Trusted advisors are adept in direct, forthright communication (including listening) skills, political astuteness, and sensitivity to the organization's culture and how things get done. They are intuitive about people and have the ability to read an audience. They are masters at being contrarian without being confrontational.

Prescience. Identifying the risks ahead requires curiosity, an ability to see matters with fresh eyes, and a willingness to question assumptions. Trusted advisors can "see around corners." They anticipate the needs of clients before the needs are even evident, and they identify issues before they arise.

Trustworthiness. Trusted advisors walk the talk, keep confidences, operate with integrity, and are obsessive about maintaining credibility with clients. They are seen as professionals who can be counted on to repeatedly take the same course of action given the same set of circumstances time after time.

Leadership. Trusted advisors often set the tone for the entire internal audit staff. They are gifted at steering others toward consensus, managing conflict, and gaining alignment on issues.

Empathy. Trusted advisors understand and focus on each stakeholder's point of view, and they are sensitive to those needs and feelings. He or she must listen. A genuine caring about others amplifies all the other qualities on this list.[5]

Interestingly, empathy ranked high in the Korn/Ferry Institute research, just as it does in most discussions on basic relationship building. Indeed, several fundamentals of relationship building show up again and again on lists developed by leadership organizations when discussing change agents.

Novarete, the ethics arm of cloud-based data services provider XSInc., cites relationship building, which it calls being a "people person," as critical: "A Change Agent's strongest asset is their strong network with solid relationships, built on trust. These same healthy relationships build the open environment that fuels positive change and inspires Change Agents. If you are approachable and kind to others, and if you actively take care of your relationships, you are operating as a Change Agent. Remember, people do not want to grow if they do not trust the person pushing the change."[6]

Michigan State University includes effective listening skills: "Effective change agents are able to explore perspectives and take them into account when looking for solutions. This will help in getting buy-in to a change; people want to feel that others are listening to their ideas. Those who do will develop stronger relationships with their people by gaining trust."[7]

Change management consultant Enclaria addresses empathy: "Change agents must be able to put themselves in other people's shoes to understand their experience. You must predict how people will feel about change even if you don't feel that way. Empathy stops you from judging people for resisting change, so you can recognize that their response to change is normal and valid."[8]

I should note that much of the research on the qualities of change agents focuses on identifying individuals who can support planned change management within an organization. Change management typically describes approaches to prepare, support, and help individuals, teams, and organizations in making organizational change. But as noted in Michigan State University's course on Strategic Leadership and Management, "Whereas change management used to primarily focus on operational and/or process improvements and cost-effectiveness, it is now something that managers are using to think about how things get done regardless of institutional hierarchy."[9]

What's more, citing an article published in the *International Journal of Management, Business, and Administration*[10], Michigan State University notes, "the success of any change effort depends heavily on the quality and workability of the relationship between the change agent and the key decision-makers within the organization."

Adding to the Ranks of Change Agents

This provides an opportunity to revisit some of the data we examined in chapter 3 regarding how internal auditors see themselves.

Internal audit leaders overwhelmingly say they support the concept of acting as change agents. Yet, only 2 in 10 poll respondents (19%) view themselves as agents of change who partner with executive management to drive change that creates value. Nearly as many (15%) say they facilitate change, but it is up to management to drive change (see **exhibit 10-1**).

This data point indicates we have far to go as a profession. Recall that the same survey showed overwhelming support among respondents for internal auditors acting as change agents (90%). Respondents also believe they have support from stakeholders, reporting that 9 in 10 (90%) board members are moderately or fully supportive and more than 3 in 4 senior managers (76%) are, as well.

So, what is holding us back? I have addressed extensively the varied facets that feed a resistance to change. I believe there are two major contributors to why so many internal auditors appear to be willing but unable to join the ranks of change agents. Most internal auditors are reactive instead of proactive, and too many are caught in what I call the *independence trap*.

Exhibit 10-1: 2 in 10 CAEs Operate as Agents of Change

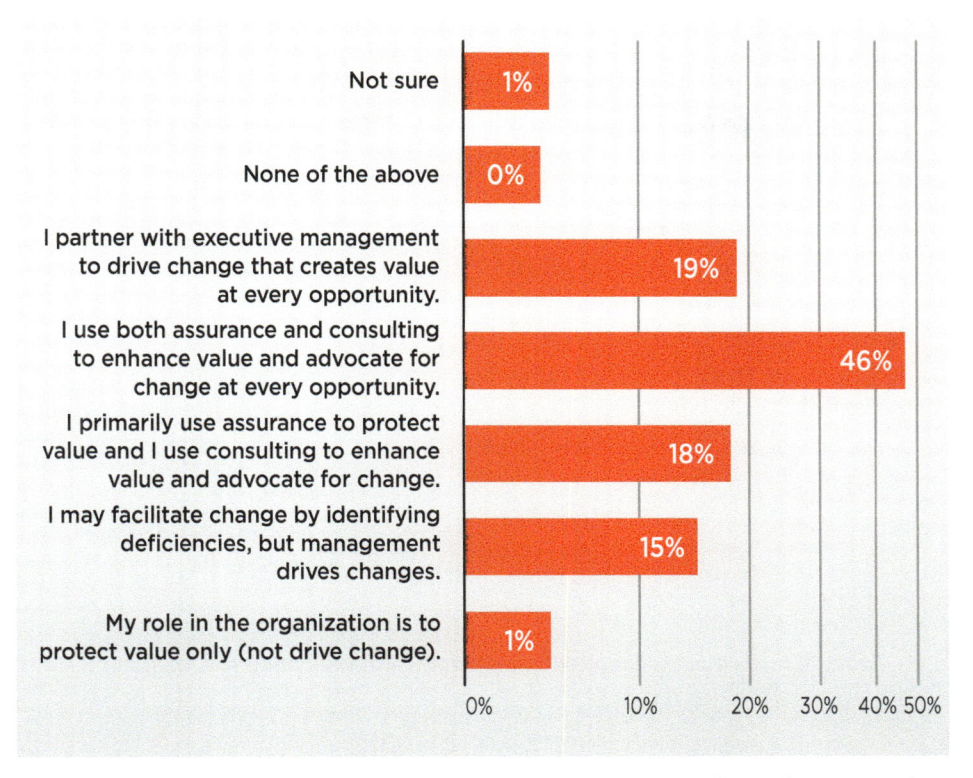

Response	Percentage
Not sure	1%
None of the above	0%
I partner with executive management to drive change that creates value at every opportunity.	19%
I use both assurance and consulting to enhance value and advocate for change at every opportunity.	46%
I primarily use assurance to protect value and I use consulting to enhance value and advocate for change.	18%
I may facilitate change by identifying deficiencies, but management drives changes.	15%
My role in the organization is to protect value only (not drive change).	1%

Note: Q12: Which one of the following statements most closely reflects your view of yourself as an Agent of Change in your organization? n = 586

Reaching Beyond Trusted Advisor

As I have mentioned, much has been said and written about the value of building relationships to advance one's career. For internal auditors, the pinnacle is reaching the lofty level of trusted advisor to our stakeholders. A trusted advisor is someone who has earned a seat at the table, is viewed as a critical part of the team, and may even achieve the level articulated in The IIA's 2030 vision statement and become "universally recognized as indispensable to effective governance, risk management, and control" within the organization.

However, as I have written throughout this book, internal auditors can no longer afford to be merely effective providers of assurance and advice. We must strive to become bold innovators for our organizations and drive positive change, especially in light of the growing speed of risk, expanding demands for effectively managing and leveraging risk, and the dire necessity to identify and anticipate emerging risks.

As noted in the discussion on the change agent value proposition (see chapter 8), change agents must strive to become catalysts for critical action. This requires becoming proactive. In other words, creating or controlling a situation by *causing something to happen* rather than responding to it afterwards.

Being proactive is a learned skill, and much has been written about the subject, primarily in addressing career development. Chrissy Scivicque, a Colorado-based career coach and corporate trainer, developed a five-step model for becoming proactive, which she published in her blog, *Eat Your Career*. In referring to the 5 P's model, she describes proactive people as "constantly moving forward, looking to the future, and making things happen. They're actively engaged, not passively observing. Being proactive is a way of thinking and acting."

This is the mindset that aspiring agents of change must embrace. Scivicque's 5 P's are:

> **Predict:** In order to be proactive, you must first develop foresight.
>
> Proactive people are rarely caught by surprise. Learn to anticipate problems and events. Understand how things work; look for patterns; recognize the regular routines, daily practices, and natural cycles that exist in your business. At the same time, don't allow yourself to become complacent. Use your imagination when anticipating future outcomes. Don't simply expect the past to always be an accurate predictor for the future; use your creativity and logic. Come up with multiple scenarios for how events could unfold. Proactive people are always on their toes.
>
> **Prevent:** Proactive people foresee potential obstacles and exert their power to find ways to overcome them before those obstacles turn into concrete roadblocks.
>
> They prevent problems that others would simply look back on in hindsight and claim unavoidable. Don't allow yourself to get swept up in a feeling of powerlessness. When challenges approach, take control and confront them head on before they grow into overwhelming problems.

Plan: Proactive people plan for the future.

Avoid one-step, "here and now" thinking and instead, look ahead and anticipate long-term consequences. Bring the future into the present; what can you do today to ensure success tomorrow? Don't make decisions in a vacuum; every decision is a link in a chain of events leading to one final conclusion. In order to make the best decision, you have to know where you came from, where you are, and where you want to end up.

Participate: Proactive people are not idle observers; they are active participants.

In order to be proactive, you must get involved. You have to take initiative and be a part of the solution. Recognize that you are only a piece of the whole and that you influence — and are influenced by — the actions of others. Don't simply react to them. Engage with them. Exert your influence and make a contribution.

Perform: Being proactive means taking timely, effective action.

You must be decisive and willing to do the work NOW. Procrastination is not an option. Take ownership of your performance and hold yourself accountable. Stand behind your decisions. Being proactive means you have taken careful, thoughtful steps to choose the appropriate path; you're not just reacting impulsively to your environment.[11]

Each of those 5 P's can be applied readily to internal auditing. Indeed, many of them are synonymous with the skills of the best internal auditors. When proactive thinking is combined with the enterprisewide perspective, internal audit practitioners are in a powerful position to be catalysts for change.

By combining well-honed proactive skills with strong business acumen, internal auditors can accomplish great things. Having a keen understanding of gaps or deficits within the organization, gleaned from their assurance and advisory engagements, these agents of change are positioned to offer solutions that drive or create value. Internal auditors who excel as change agents are not afraid of revolutionary change. They are not timid. They speak up. If they see the potential to do something bold and decisive, they do it.

The Independence Trap

Throughout *Agents of Change*, I have referenced how the profession's focus on independence and objectivity can sometimes hinder advocacy for change. It doesn't have to. Agents of change are masters at the art of proactively driving change while maintaining independence and objectivity. Internal auditors striving to become change agents must become comfortable with this concept.

From early on, whether in university studies or early in our careers, internal auditors are indoctrinated to embrace and protect our independence and objectivity at all costs. Indeed, the heroes in our profession are those who muster the courage and integrity to battle those who would dare to tamper with them. Let me state clearly that I agree and wholeheartedly support this. Independence and objectivity are bedrock for providing effective internal audit assurance and advisory services that are critical to overall good governance.

But blind allegiance to those concepts can impede serving our organizations well. Admittedly, it is easier to accept and rigidly stick to simple constructs of complex concepts than to try to understand the details and nuances that drive them. However, the inherent danger in blind allegiance is that little in our professional or personal lives is a simple yes or no, good or bad, all or nothing. Agents of change must successfully deconstruct the details and nuances behind the profession's focus on independence and objectivity, and in doing so attain a greater understanding and appreciation of both.

Let's turn to the primary source of our connection to independence and objectivity — the *Standards*. Three standards apply in this context, Standard 1100 – Independence and Objectivity, Standard 1120 – Individual Objectivity, and 1130 – Impairment to Independence or Objectivity. Let's examine them in detail.

Standard 1100 – Independence and Objectivity states, "The internal audit activity must be independent, and internal auditors must be objective in performing their work."

If we break down the two concepts, we should first note that independence relates to the internal audit activity, and objectivity applies to individual internal auditors. In the context of practitioners acting as agents of change, this all but eliminates discussion of independence (don't worry, I will revisit the issue of independence later in this chapter). Let's focus first on what the *Standards* say about objectivity. From the interpretation of Standard 1100 – Independence and Objectivity:

> *Objectivity is an unbiased mental attitude that allows internal auditors to perform engagements in such a manner that they believe in their work product and that no quality compromises are made. Objectivity requires that internal auditors do not subordinate their judgment on audit matters to others. Threats to objectivity must be managed at the individual auditor, engagement, functional, and organizational levels.*

This interpretation focuses on ensuring that internal auditors perform with the singular goal of producing work that is of the highest quality and not compromised by influences or factors that do not relate directly to the engagement. In addition, it makes the individual auditor's judgment the primary driver for that work.

Frankly, I have never believed that an objectivity impairment can occur unless and until an internal auditor is called upon to provide assurance on some aspect of work for which they were previously responsible. So, I believe there is no objectivity impairment where we are providing advice or advocating for change, as long as we believe in our work product and no compromises are made in quality. The objectivity standard is primarily to protect the integrity of internal auditors' assurance work — not to prevent our engagement where the organization truly needs our expertise.

Standard 1120 – Individual Objectivity states, "Internal auditors must have an impartial, unbiased attitude and avoid any conflicts of interest." This is where internal auditors may have a legitimate cause for concern when providing advice or advocating for change.

The *Standard's* interpretation for individual objectivity addresses conflict of interest as *a situation in which an internal auditor, who is in a position of trust, has a competing professional or personal interest.* It goes on to state: *A conflict of interest can create an appearance of impropriety that can undermine confidence in the internal auditor, the internal audit activity, and the profession. A conflict of interest could impair an individual's ability to perform his or her duties and responsibilities objectively.*

Let's address each of these. All internal auditors, by definition, are working for the good of the organization. Furthermore, the Mission of Internal Audit directs practitioners, "To enhance and protect organizational value by providing risk-based and objective assurance, advice, and insight." Agents of change who leverage their position, relationships, knowledge, innovation, and proactive mindset to create positive change are fulfilling the mission at the highest levels. As long as the internal auditor acts to protect and enhance organizational value, there is no "competing or personal interest."

To avoid any "appearance of impropriety," agents of change must remain cognizant of their actions and interactions with stakeholders and make it clear that their dedication to providing unbiased assurance and advice is paramount. This can be achieved even while driving positive change in the organization. In the end, the CAE must be the guardian of objectivity for the members of the internal audit team. If an internal auditor has played an advisory role that resulted in change to business operations, the CAE should ensure that the same internal auditor is not subsequently assigned to an assurance engagement whose scope includes the implementation of advice or change offered by the internal auditor. If the CAE believes that the entire internal audit team may have an objectivity impairment as a result of advice advocated by the team, he or she should bring in a third party to undertake any subsequent assurance engagements.

Standard 1130 – Impairment to Independence or Objectivity directs practitioners on proper disclosures when an impairment of independence or objectivity is suspected. The interpretation lists examples of impairment that may include *personal conflict of interest, scope limitations, restrictions on access to records, personnel, and properties, and resources limitations, such as funding*. The majority of examples in the interpretation address independence.

The supplemental Standards 1130.A1, 1130.A2, 1130.A3, 1130.C1, and 1130.C2 anticipate the potential for conflicts based on specific assurance and consulting scenarios.

As noted, Standard 1130 – Impairment to Independence or Objectivity and its subcategories focus on mitigating impacts of suspected impairment. Ultimately, practitioners who strive to become agents of change must keep two things in mind:

- Remain true to the *Standards* on objectivity.
- When driving change, never take on the role of decision-maker.

Independence Does Not Mean Isolation

I wanted to end this chapter by examining how the importance of internal audit independence can sometimes be misconstrued to the detriment of the profession. We should first put internal audit independence in its proper perspective. Again, let's turn to the *Standards* to begin the discussion. Standard 1100 – Independence and Objectivity states simply that the internal audit activity must be independent.

The interpretation adds clarity to this direction:

> *Independence is the freedom from conditions that threaten the ability of the internal audit activity to carry out internal audit responsibilities in an unbiased manner. To achieve the degree of independence necessary to effectively carry out the responsibilities of the internal audit activity, the chief audit executive has direct and unrestricted access to senior management and the board. This can be achieved through a dual-reporting relationship. Threats to independence must be managed at the individual auditor, engagement, functional, and organizational levels.*

Therefore, internal audit independence is tied primarily to three things: 1) freedom from conditions that threaten internal audit's unbiased assurance and advisory services, 2) direct and unrestricted access to senior management and the board, and 3) a recommended dual-reporting relationship.

As noted earlier, Standard 1130 – Impairment to Independence or Objectivity addresses how practitioners should alert stakeholders to impairment. There are genuine and serious threats to independence that can be created by scope limitations; restrictions on access to records, personnel, and properties; and resources limitations, such as funding.

Over my career, I have witnessed and written about attempts by misguided or nefarious senior managers to control or limit internal audit by tightening the purse strings, manipulating its agenda, dictating its scope of work, blocking access to information or the board, and even physical intimidation. These are genuine and troubling examples of real threats to internal audit independence.

However, the answer to such threats is not to try to protect the function through separation and isolation. If anything, such defensive posturing makes internal audit only that much more mysterious, less understood, and undervalued.

The IIA's Three Lines Model provides excellent perspective on this point. The model's principles-based approach is designed to deliver clarity and greater flexibility about the roles of the three key players in risk management — governing bodies (boards), executive management, and internal audit.

These areas of responsibility are generally described as:

Accountability by the governing body to stakeholders for oversight.

Actions (including managing risk) by management to achieve organizational objectives.

Assurance and advice by an independent internal audit function to provide insight, confidence, and encouragement for continuous improvement.

Some have argued that internal audit should remain ensconced in the "third line" out of an abundance of caution to ensure its independence and the objectivity of its staff. However, the refreshed model released in 2020 clearly emphasizes that "independence does not imply isolation."

"There must be regular interaction between internal audit and management. . . . There is a need for collaboration and communication across both the first- and second-line roles of management and internal audit," according to the revised model.

For me, there are two key lessons to take away from this discussion. First, stronger relationships build stronger communication and alignment, which benefit risk management and governance overall. Second, building relationships with stakeholders helps them better understand the value of independent and objective assurance and advice and ultimately do more to protect internal audit's independence and objectivity than to compromise it.

CHAPTER 11
The Innovative Mindset

Innovation is the ability to see change as an opportunity, not a threat.

— Steve Jobs —

It is highly appropriate to begin a discussion about innovation with a quote from Steve Jobs, the late chairman, CEO, and co-founder of Apple Inc. The number of revolutionary inventions that have sprung from Apple's innovation hub in Cupertino, California, is truly astounding, especially considering they took place in a span of about 25 years.

From iPods to iPads, from iTunes to the Apple Watch, from the Macintosh personal computer to the ubiquitous iPhone, Apple's breakthroughs in computing, music, and entertainment are synonymous with these industries today. Indeed, the assembly line of invention from Apple has fundamentally changed the way we work, live, and play. The world lost one of the greatest innovators of the 20th century far too soon when Jobs succumbed to pancreatic cancer in 2011 at age 56. What he left behind is a company whose culture is steeped in innovation, and one that is the envy of the corporate world.

Of course, trying to replicate Apple's success by simply announcing, "We will be innovative starting today," is foolish. Jobs was able to instill an innovative mindset in his organization over time that was driven by his outsized personality and force of will. There have been numerous published accounts of his rudeness and outright cruelty to those he viewed as getting in the way of what he wanted. However, in the end, he succeeded in building an organization that thrives on change. Those who successfully innovate must embrace change, and those who seek to drive change must have an innovative spirit. To be sure, to innovate is to make changes in something established, especially by introducing new methods, ideas, or products. Therefore, agents of change must innovate. That is not to say they must possess innate skills to invent new, revolutionary products. Instead, they must have a deep and intuitive understanding of how change creates value.

Prepare Yourself for Innovation

Innovative thinking does not come naturally, especially for those of us in internal auditing. If you're not an innovator, don't feel badly; you are not alone. Traditional education systems focus on teaching through lecturing and learning by listening. They measure achievement in test scores rather than examination and debate. While such long-held, global teaching practices do not openly discourage innovation, they don't do much to nurture it. But what would happen if we began with a different proposition? What if we could unleash the potential of anyone to innovate?

That is precisely what Ami Dror did when he and his partners began a company called LeapLearner in Shanghai, according to a recent *Forbes* article. The company taught children computer code and challenged them to create a video game. Dror's central premise was that the trial-and-error process of writing lines of code and testing them by hitting "execute" would help break down barriers to innovation. We can take three valuable lessons from LeapLearner's approach.

> **Free yourself from the fear of failure.** Coding allows for almost instantaneous feedback, which creates a comfort level with asking and receiving feedback and direction. It also helps with developing critical thinking and problem-solving skills, all while teaching children to innovate.
>
> **Create a culture where innovation is rewarded.** The LeapLearner process has a built-in reward. Successful innovation equals a cool new video game. In addition, Dror encourages innovation as an employer by rewarding employees who take risks.
>
> **Make risk-taking a more consistent behavior.** This concept may be anathema to many in a profession centered on managing risk, but it is critical to breaking away from traditional approaches that often dissuade asking for feedback and rewarding risk taking and "outside-the-box" thinking.

Dror received a significant affirmation for his approach to innovation just three years after opening the doors at LeapLearner. He was awarded China's prestigious Yicai Brilliant prize in 2018 as one of that nation's top entrepreneurs.

"My core innovation principles are very simple no matter if I share it with my students, my employees, or my kids," Dror told *Forbes*. "Have more dreams than achievements. Chase your dreams as fast as you can, and fail fast if needed, but always, always ask 'Why?'"[1]

Dror's final point should resonate with internal auditors. Every practitioner's toolbox must include that simple but powerful three-letter word — why.

In *Trusted Advisors*, I examined in depth 10 characteristics of outstanding internal auditors. These were the keys that helped elevate top performers in our profession to the vaunted level of trusted advisor. As I discussed in chapter 9, one of the characteristics was open-mindedness, which is particularly relevant to being innovative. In reviewing the chapter on open-mindedness, I was struck with how much it focused on being open to change and innovation. From *Trusted Advisors*:

> "Open-mindedness can be deeply challenged by change. Rather than simply being open to change and riding it out, outstanding internal auditors are typically agents of change. They create buy-in, motivate action, maintain momentum, and establish a sense of urgency even when management may have other priorities. If you believe, as I do, that internal audit can bring about positive change, you must embrace change not only in what you do but how you do it.
>
> This ties in with stakeholder expectations, which have shifted over time. Boards and audit committees now expect internal auditors to follow the risks. So, when new risks emerge or old risks rear their ugly heads (and they do regularly), their expectations of us transform accordingly. As I noted in *Lessons Learned on the Audit Trail*, our stakeholders ultimately judge our value. I would also add that it is our stakeholders who will ultimately decide the extent to which we are trusted advisors.
>
> Being open to change enables us to have a hand in choosing what we want change to look like. That is pretty powerful stuff, but it doesn't come without a significant threat — complacency. The minute we become complacent and think we know everything there is to know about internal auditing, the risks we audit, and feel we no longer need to invest in learning and growing, we cease to be an outstanding internal auditor or an agent of change. And we will certainly never step into or sustain the role of trusted advisor."[2]

In the same chapter, I shared some important experiences about practices and habits that can act against open-mindedness. It manifested itself in a list of things not to do, and should be on the wall of every internal auditor seeking to be a change agent:

Don't dwell on the past. How likely is it that people will seek your advice if you tell them only how things used to be done? They may find the information interesting from a strictly historical perspective, but ultimately, they need help knowing what to do right now, in six months, or next year. If you're not able to envision what the future looks like from your client's point of view, your client won't view you as a valuable resource. Over time we have seen many innovations that enable internal audit to adapt and maintain or become more valuable. Technology is a good example because it multiplies our capacity to an extraordinary degree. If we focus on old ways of conducting an audit, we will be unable to audit at the speed of risk and will quickly lose credibility and stature as a trusted resource.

Don't shrink from getting to the bottom of issues. You will always struggle to find the root cause of an issue if you are not open-minded. I have seen internal auditors arrive at the end of the audit process and still display a stunning lack of understanding of the issue. For example, they may report a condition (a failure in a control in a certain area) and an unsupported, under-researched cause (the people in that area are not adequately trained), then provide an underwhelming or painfully obvious recommendation (do a better job training). Well, that may look fine, albeit uninspiring, on the surface. But what if the cause that was articulated wasn't the true root cause of the control failure? Perhaps there was no reinforcement mechanism in place to drive employees to follow company policies. Or maybe culture was the culprit; possibly the prevailing corporate philosophy was one of the ends justifying the means, thereby excusing the lack of effective controls. The point is, if you are complacent and not open to digging deeper, you are unlikely to get to the root cause and, as a consequence, your value will be significantly diminished.

Don't take a myopic view in making recommendations. The easy solution may be right, but it also may not. In many instances, if the obvious solution was the right one, chances are that it would have already been conceived and implemented. It's best to assume there is a reason that solution isn't already in place; maybe it has been tried and abandoned because of a lack of success, or it wasn't assessed as a critical enough risk to even test the solution. Open-mindedness calls for creativity — being willing to explore alternative explanations for why something happened and proposing creative solutions for ensuring it doesn't happen again. Of course, there is some risk to this approach. Lars Christensen reminds us that there are people who will mistake internal audit's guidance or recommendation for creative solutions as "approval by the auditors" to do what they want. This should not cause us to abandon creativity, however; we simply have to be prepared to defend our recommendations with as much creativity as we used to develop them.

Don't neglect to seek input from those you are auditing. Internal auditors are often compared, rarely flatteringly, with police officers. So, let's imagine a police officer stops you for speeding and prepares to give you a ticket. You respond by suggesting that the two of you work together to find a different solution, rather than a ticket. While the officer would probably be disinclined to consider such an option, this is metaphorically what internal auditors must sometimes be willing to do in their audits.

One of the AEC survey respondents pointed out how critical this aspect of open-mindedness is to an activity in which internal auditors participate on a regular basis — negotiation. Effective negotiation means not automatically imposing your own solution when another may be just as good or better; it is based on an appreciation for what can be achieved if we are open to alternatives. We must be willing to hear our clients' views, discuss them, and work toward a mutually acceptable solution.

Don't view the world in black and white. There are often multiple paths to the same outcome. Outstanding internal auditors explore these paths, discuss their advantages and disadvantages, and assess their risk. An ability to navigate ambiguity was specifically called out by one of the AEC survey respondents who described it as "comfort and skill in dealing with competing truths." I like that particular definition because it seems especially pertinent to internal auditing. The ability to see beyond black and white ties in with a point I made on ethical resiliency in chapter 2 — the need to leave preconceived notions at the door. Never enter an audit with your findings, solutions, or opinion of the involved parties already in mind.[3]

Learning to Innovate

What steps can we take to become more innovative? Mikael Eriksson Björling knows a thing or two about innovation, and he's passionate about it. Indeed, his title at the Ericsson Networked Society Lab is Networked Society *Evangelist*. Björling, whose work at the lab supports creation of "networked societies," believes most innovation is directly or indirectly driven by new technology. So, understanding new technology and its impact is an essential prerequisite to innovation.

Björling authored a series of blog posts for the Networked Society Lab about innovation that capture key steps to creating an innovative mindset.[4] I'll share an abbreviated version of those posts here and discuss how Björling's insights can be applied by agents of change within their organizations.

Be open to change. This concept has already been thoroughly discussed, but Björling adds an admonition to remain curious about the constant state of transformation by keeping track of change and new technology and constantly analyzing the real and potential consequences of transformative change. From an internal audit perspective, Björling's direction describes concisely how practitioners should view the way their organizations are embracing new technologies. Earlier, I concluded that internal auditors must "understand the business" of their organizations, but I could expand that to emphasize that internal auditors must "understand the business and the technology that enables value creation."

Embrace creativity. Björling makes the case that creativity replaces traditional scientific method in an innovative mindset. This argument is predominant among many who have successfully practiced innovation in the realm of daily business activities. This innovation-as-art approach — versus innovation as science — doesn't rule out the need for structure, process, and methodology. All are required for innovation. However, it begins with the premise that creativity rather than process is the starting point for innovation.

That may be particularly challenging for internal auditors. The very definition of the profession describes a "systematic, disciplined approach." However, a differentiator between those who are followers in our profession from those who are innovators may well be a creative mindset. We can certainly be technically sound and creative at the same time.

Think big. Innovation is more than just incremental improvements to existing products. Innovation requires the ability and courage to think beyond the normal or status quo. Björling argues that big thinking and innovation combine analytical skills, entrepreneurial spirit, and the ability to fantasize. I have already addressed the first two skills, but few associate fantasizing with work. Indeed, the very definition of fantasizing — to indulge in daydreaming about something desired — includes negative connotations associated with *indulging* and *daydreaming*.

It should not be surprising that internal auditors, whose processes are steeped in traditional scientific method, rarely nurture such behaviors as part of their professional development. Björling suggests big thinking is more easily achieved in diverse organizational cultures versus "homogenous groups that are likely to reproduce versions of similar thinking over and over again."[5]

Be courageous. Björling eloquently writes, "It takes courage not to conform to widespread beliefs and popular 'truths' in big organizations. It takes courage to challenge proven strategies and successful products and services before they go into decline. It takes courage to question management and colleagues for doing things the way they have always done. It takes courage to constantly problematize and be that one person who always goes against the grain and tries to think about things from a different angle. It takes courage to be vulnerable rather than playing it safe according to established business practice. It takes courage to venture into the new and uncertain, risking failure."

We often speak of the need for internal auditors to be courageous in executing their role. However, we are typically speaking of the courage to highlight what isn't working or what is wrong. Björling is speaking about the courage to identify what might be. While it can be intimidating and frightening, risk-taking is critical to innovation. Innovation doesn't happen when people *dare to be the same.*

Think and act fast. One of the most difficult aspects of change is overcoming the reluctance to act. Those with an innovative mindset learn not just to set that reluctance aside but to understand intuitively that innovation requires a fast-moving process to keep up with change. I speak extensively about auditing at the *speed of risk*. Change agents must *innovate at the speed of change.*

This is not an easy concept for most people to grasp. That's primarily because humans are linear thinkers and change driven by technology is moving at an exponential rate. I addressed the challenges of exponential thinking in my blog, *Chambers on the Profession*, by quoting celebrated entrepreneur, innovator, and founder and chairman of the X Prize Foundation, Peter Diamandis. He addresses exponential change using a simple explanation:

> 30 linear steps @ 1 meter per step = 30 meters
>
> 30 exponential steps @ 1 meter (1, 2, 4, 8, 16, 32, 64, 128, etc.) = 1,073,741,824 meters

Björling notes that twentieth century innovation was typically a slow process, with product concepts going from the drawing board to the showroom in a span of years! With advanced technology in 3D printing and virtual reality-assisted design and manufacturing, that process has been shrunk to a matter of months or weeks. In addition to acting fast, Björling references the need to fail fast.

"In this context, it's also critical to adhere to the notion of 'failing fast,' as new ideas and concepts have to be tested out quickly and be shut down just as quickly if they don't fly. In this way, the organization can move resources to the next concept instead of getting stuck in a dead-end innovation project, because after all, the world's next 'big idea' is just around the corner."[6]

I believe this aspect of innovation is significant enough to merit its own step.

Fail fast, fail gracefully. Daniel Burrus, an innovation expert and futurist, notes that no matter the exponential speed of change and innovation, the statistical relationship between failure and innovation remains consistent. "Studies have shown it can take upward of 3,000 ideas to produce one product or service that goes on to be a commercial success. It is rare to capture lightning in a bottle instantaneously these days without that same rate of failure of the past."[7]

As with the LeapLearning teaching method, there's a value in failure if it leads to an eventual successful outcome. That is why failing fast is a must. "Failing fast allows you to move on from that missed shot much sooner so you can get to the next effort, which will yield better results," according to Burrus.[8]

As internal auditors, we are programmed to be averse to failure. So, embracing the idea that there is value in failure is a challenge for many in our profession. Yet, to be innovative change agents, we must accept that failure is a risk that comes with innovation and change. By understanding that failure is part and parcel to innovation, we also should refrain from seeking blame or pointing fingers when an innovative effort falls short.

I could devote entire chapters to each of the six topics covered in this section. To be sure, the art of innovation and creativity has launched the careers of countless inventors, psychologists, artists, not to mention art critics. These six elements provide a sound beginning to our investigation of innovation. As I mentioned earlier, it is foolish to think we can become innovative overnight. But, as with anything of value, an innovative mindset is something to strive for and a critical tool in the change agent's toolbox.

Why Innovation for Internal Audit?

Throughout *Agents of Change*, I have made the case that not only can internal audit drive positive change in the organization it serves, but internal audit itself must undergo a fundamental change to bring this about. As the demands grow on organizations to be more flexible and resilient in the face of accelerating technological disruption, opportunities and risk abound. Those who develop the skills to become agents of change will be the ones who not only identify and provide assurance on those risks, but also those who help their organizations exploit the opportunities.

The value of having change agents on the payroll is becoming increasingly evident. There is growing demand from the C-suite for informed, innovative ideas that support decisive and positive action and change.

A key finding from an IBM report published in the midst of the COVID-19 pandemic supports the premise. The report from the Institute for Business Value identified an evolution in thinking by senior management on how business would operate in a post-pandemic world. "Leaders are expecting more from their transformation initiatives. They identify competitiveness and workforce resilience as the benefits they most want from ongoing digital transformation."[9]

One of the senior management epiphanies identified in "COVID-19 and the Future of Business" was that "traumatic stress has hijacked corporate strategy."

"Executives are tasked with defining their organizations' vision. But it can be hard to focus if they are continually putting out fires. While workforce safety and resilience, cost management, and organization agility emerge as top priorities for the short- and longer-term, the pandemic has amplified old business fears and introduced new ones. The result? Executives are enamored with the priority du jour."[10]

If senior management is indeed hyper-focused on issues of the day, internal audit must be able to deliver the immediacy, resilience, agility, and innovation that will demand.

A Final Thought on Innovation

Being in an atmosphere where innovation, creativity, and change can thrive is incredibly fulfilling. Several times in my career I have found myself in such a position and was able to make real change. Throughout my professional life, I also have strived to be open to new opportunities, new adventures, and new perspectives. Like many others, I have a healthy respect for career opportunities with all their commensurate benefits. But I have always been driven by much more. When I grew weary in a position, I knew I was no longer learning or growing. I refused to be caught in a rut, and even left a higher-paying position simply because it was ceaselessly routine and mundane.

I frequently advise young internal auditors to not be afraid to move to another company, or even leave the profession for a while and return when recharged. If you lose the spark, energy, drive, or innovative mindset, your effectiveness as a change agent wanes.

CONCLUSION
Agents of the Future

— • • • • —

There is nothing permanent except change.

— Heraclitus —

Over my long and gratifying career in internal auditing, I have witnessed great strides as the profession has repeatedly pivoted to react and adapt to each challenge that has come its way. The profession's journey is impressive and inspiring. We have gone from providing accounting-focused assurance over financial controls to offering assurance related to the full portfolio of risks by leveraging hindsight, insight, and foresight. Indeed, it could be argued that we have progressed from being mere "counters of change" to positioning ourselves as "agents of change."

Throughout this book, I examined internal auditing's evolution, from its origins centuries ago to today's modern profession, and the arc of that history has indeed been much more evolution than revolution. That must change. We can no longer afford the comfort of only responding or reacting. We must be proactive. The forces that control modern business, economies, and societies demand agility and resilience, and our organizations deserve nothing less from us. Internal audit must be on the forefront of change.

Fueled by technology and disruption, the pace of transformation today is accelerating to a point of turmoil. Yet, throughout history, those two factors have been ever-present as catalysts for change. Familiar epochs driven by technological disruption are part of the lexicon of human achievement — the Bronze Age, the Renaissance, the Industrial Revolution, the Atomic Age, and the Digital Age.

We must take heart and inspiration from the times in which we live and rise to the challenges of a world undergoing exponential change.

Revolutionary Evolution

Beyond its context in government or military terms, the word *revolution* describes a dramatic and wide-reaching change in the way something works or is organized, or in people's ideas about it. In contrast, the word *evolution* is the gradual development of something, especially from a simple to a more complex form. While seemingly contradictory, the two concepts can be combined. *Revolutionary evolution* describes a dramatic and wide-reaching change to a more complex form. This is what is necessary for internal audit, and the leaders of this revolutionary evolution are the agents of change among us, as well as the agents of the future.

Agents of Change has addressed key aspects of what that revolutionary evolution must entail. They include:

- Transforming our mindsets to thrive in an era in which change is fast-paced, dynamic, and unrelenting.
- Acknowledging our shortcomings as a profession and as individual practitioners — and committing to improve them.
- Letting go of comfortable, outdated processes and accepting radical ways of thinking.
- Embracing technology in the way we undertake our mission and as a focus of our mission.
- Expanding our skillsets in communication, innovation, and proactive thinking.
- Viewing independence and objectivity as tools for change — not barriers.
- Willingly taking on the mantle of agents of change.

Throughout history, successful revolutionaries have been those who could inspire and enact radical change. The characteristics of those revolutionary leaders and the tactics they used to inspire change have been thoroughly examined. We can look to those studies to inspire our own revolutionary evolution. Inspiring Leadership Now, a leadership training organization, makes it its business to know and understand revolutionary thinking. It offers 10 ways to become a "powerful voice for change." By now, the items from that list — condensed below — should start to sound familiar.

1. **Use your voice and speak out.** Your voice is the spark to potentially ignite the fire of change.
2. **Take a step.** The biggest thing in starting a motion for change is taking the first step.
3. **Communication.** Articulate your vision. What do you want to accomplish and why?
4. **Tell the story.** Behind every movement for change there is a story. It's the story that enables others to rally around a common purpose.
5. **Be bold. Be innovative.** Movement starters are those who say, "There must be more that we can do."
6. **Use setbacks.** Leverage failures as learning opportunities, not as deal breakers.
7. **Gain skills as you go.** Start small and grow your skill base.
8. **Stay focused.** Make it your mission to hone your focus on what it is you want to see, and build your determination through accepting the challenges that come your way.
9. **Generate and appreciate your followers.** If you are the spark for change, your supporters are the kindling for your fire. Encouraging and supporting your followers is key to generating momentum.
10. **Remember the big picture — and the little guys.** People care about purpose. Let this allow your movement to inspire change and gain momentum.[1]

Agents of Change Are Among Us

Throughout this book, I have shared the thoughts of several internal audit leaders who have embraced the change-agent attitude and leveraged it for success. Their observations and counsel about courage, innovation, communication, and relevance provide ample inspiration for applying the change agent mindset to our work as internal auditors. Importantly, we must realize that there are many would-be change agents who have yet to reach the highest levels, particularly those among the newest members of our profession.

An *Internal Auditor* magazine article on its 2020 class of "Emerging Leaders" speaks clearly to these young professionals already being equipped with the change-agent mindset.

> "Emerging Leaders extol internal audit's access to all levels of an organization and its role in strategic planning. Even at relatively early stages in their careers, they're already earning seats at the proverbial table. And those seats are earned based on both their mastery of internal audit processes and their ability to see the bigger picture. As a result, they report leading massive international engagements, jumping into complicated situations on short notice, and starting up audit functions at far-flung branches of their organizations. Adeptness with data is a given with this group. No longer is data analytics a sought-after specialty — this year's class fiddles with numbers for fun, and many write software suited to their department's specific needs on technology and the requisite skills to support it."[2]

That description of the young internal audit leaders (all 30 years old or younger) gives me great hope that the newest crop of internal auditors are keen to embrace the change-agent mindset and, in some ways, are better equipped to assume the mantle. This does not mean those who have worked in the profession for longer periods are unable to achieve such forward-looking greatness. However, they should look at their younger colleagues as potential mentors for guidance in leveraging technology, innovation, and process change.

Remaining True to the Profession

Our definition of revolutionary evolution describes "a dramatic and wide-reaching change to a more complex form." What it doesn't describe is abandoning or rewriting the fundamentals of the profession. What has made internal auditing one of the greatest professions — and one on the cusp of being even greater — are its core principles. Even as we strive to become agents of change, our focus and commitment to our core principles — integrity, competence, objectivity, alignment, quality, self-improvement, communications, insights, being proactive, and promoting improvement within the organizations we serve — must never waver. Indeed, following the core principles is part of the formula for success.

Successful agents of change understand that the change we promote and drive within our organizations must be enabled by our other work. Internal auditors exist to serve their organizations with assurance and advice, and only when we consistently provide those services at the highest levels can we become agents of change.

But don't confuse efficiency or adopting new processes with being change agents. It is not about finding new ways to generate a report. It is not about becoming an IT expert or learning to write code. It is not even about being the cleverest or the most innovative person in the room. It is about embracing a way of life that continuously seeks positive change. Change is not a process — it is an outcome.

The Constancy of Change

The quote from the Greek philosopher Heraclitus that opens this chapter provides a good close to this book and a good beginning to your journey as an agent of change. Change is constant, Heraclitus judged, change is the only thing that is permanent. He also is credited with the aphorism, "No man steps in the same river twice." This fits with his fundamental premise, because the river and the man are constantly changing. Today the river is a raging torrent of change, and we as agents of change must help guide our organizations safely across it.

Go forth and be an agent of change!

Notes

CHAPTER 1
An Evolving Profession

1. B. Bernstein, *Against the Gods: The Remarkable Story of Risk* (New York, NY: John Wiley & Sons, Inc., 1996).
2. S. Ramamoorti, *Internal Auditing: History, Evolution, and Prospects* (Lake Mary, FL: Internal Audit Foundation, 2003).
3. James L. Boockholdt, "Historical perspective on the auditor's role: The early experience of the American railroads," *Accounting Historians Journal*, Volume 10: Issue 1, Article 4 (1983), https://egrove.olemiss.edu/aah_journal/vol10/iss1/4
4. Ibid.
5. Ibid.
6. *Internal Auditing: History, Evolution, and Prospects*.
7. Ibid.
8. Ibid.
9. *2020 North American Pulse of Internal Audit: Bridging Critical Gaps* (Lake Mary, FL: The Institute of Internal Auditors, 2020).
10. *Enterprise Risk Management – Integrated Framework* (Committee of Sponsoring Organizations of the Treadway Commission, 2017).

CHAPTER 2
The Imperative for Change

1. *Exploring the Next Generation of Internal Auditing*, Protiviti, 2020, https://www.protiviti.com/sites/default/files/2020-ia-capabilities-needs-survey-protiviti.pdf
2. *Internal Audit Capabilities and Needs survey, Embracing the Next Generation of Internal Auditing*, Protiviti, 2019, https://www.protiviti.com/sites/default/files/united_states/insights/2019-ia-capabilities-and-needs-survey-protiviti.pdf
3. *Embracing the Next Generation of Internal Auditing*, Protiviti, 2019, 27, https://www.protiviti.com/sites/default/files/united_states/insights/2019-ia-capabilities-and-needs-survey-protiviti.pdf
4. *State of the Internal Audit Profession Report, Elevating Internal Audit's Role: The Digitally Fit Function*, PwC, 2020, https://www.pwc.com/sg/en/publications/assets/state-of-the-internal-audit-2019.pdf
5. Rosabeth Moss Kanter, "10 Reasons Why People Resist Change," *Harvard Business Review* (Sept. 25, 2012), https://hbr.org/2012/09/ten-reasons-people-resist-chang
6. The IIA Global Strategic Plan (Lake Mary, FL: The Institute of Internal Auditors, 2019–23).

7. *North American Pulse of Internal Audit: The Internal Audit Transformation Imperative* (Lake Mary, FL: The Institute of Internal Auditors, 2018).
8. *AGILE INTERNAL AUDIT: Leading practices on the journey to becoming Agile*, Global Knowledge Brief (Lake Mary, FL: The Institute of Internal Auditors, 2019).

CHAPTER 3
Independence Doesn't Imply Isolation

1. Timothy Berichon, *Ready and Relevant: Prepare to Audit What Matters Most* (Lake Mary, FL: Internal Audit Foundation, 2020).
2. Richard Branson, located and accessed on many sites, including pinterest.com, me.me, twitter, and quotestats.com.
3. S. Ramamoorti, *Internal Auditing: History, Evolution, and Prospects* (Lake Mary, FL: Internal Audit Foundation, 2003).
4. Ibid.
5. *International Standards for the Professional Practice of Internal Auditing* (Lake Mary, FL: The Institute of internal Auditors, 2017).
6. Ibid.
7. Ibid.
8. Ibid.
9. E. Whiteacre Jr., http://www.brainyquote.com/quotes/quotes/e/edward-whit516604.html

CHAPTER 4
Agent Change Thyself

1. E. D. Hirsch Jr., Joseph F. Kett, and James Trefil, eds. (2002). "Physician, heal thyself." *The New Dictionary of Cultural Literacy* (Boston: Houghton Mifflin).
2. *2018 North American Pulse of Internal Audit: The Internal Audit Transformation Imperative* (Lake Mary, FL: The Institute of Internal Auditors, 2018), 7.
3. Ibid, 11.
4. *2019 North American Pulse of Internal Audit: Defining Alignment in a Dynamic Risk Landscape* (Lake Mary, FL: The Institute of Internal Auditors, 2018), 17.
5. S. Urban, "The innovative internal auditor," *Internal Auditor* (June 2017): 49.
6. "Times Call for Liberal Action, Says Kennedy," Lodi (Calif.) *News-Sentinel*, May 13, 1961, 3.
7. *Agile Auditing: Transforming the Internal Audit Process*, Executive Summary (Lake Mary, FL: Internal Audit Foundation, 2020), 4.
8. Ibid.
9. International Professional Practices Framework (IPPF) (Lake Mary, FL: The Institute of Internal Auditors, 2017), 58–59.
10. Government Auditing Standards, 2018 Revision, U.S. Government Accountability Office, GAO-18-568G (Washington, D.C.: 2018), 191.
11. *2019 North American Pulse of Internal Audit: Defining Alignment in a Dynamic Risk Landscape*, 8.
12. Ibid, 11.

13. Ibid.
14. "The Road Ahead for Internal Audit: 5 Bold Predictions for the 2020s," *Chambers on the Profession, Internal Auditor* (Nov. 4, 2019).
15. "Leveraging an innovative internal audit strategy to sell your story of value," *Resilient* podcast (New York, NY: Deloitte, 2020). https://www2.deloitte.com/us/en/pages/advisory/articles/resilient-kenneth-chen-internal-audit-relationship-with-management.html

CHAPTER 5
Driving Change Means Being Agile

1. Richard F. Chambers, *The Speed of Risk: Lessons Learned on the Audit Trail*, 2nd Edition (Lake Mary, FL: Internal Audit Foundation, 2019), 22.
2. "What is Agile Auditing? The Benefits of Taking Your Audit Team Agile," AuditBoard. Accessed at: https://www.auditboard.com/blog/what-is-agile-auditing-benefits/
3. Ibid.
4. "Becoming Agile: A guide to elevating internal audit's performance and value, Part 1: Understanding Agile Internal Audit," Deloitte. Accessed at: https://www2.deloitte.com/us/en/pages/advisory/articles/agile-internal-audit-planning-performance-value.html
5. Ibid.
6. Ibid.
7. Rick A. Wright, *Agile Auditing: Transforming the Internal Audit Process* (Lake Mary, FL: Internal Audit Foundation, 2019).
8. "What is Agile Auditing? The Benefits of Taking Your Audit Team Agile."
9. "Adopting Agile Projects – Your grandfather's audit won't work here!" Deloitte. Accessed at: https://www2.deloitte.com/content/dam/Deloitte/us/Documents/risk/us-risk-auditing-agile-projects.pdf

CHAPTER 6
Leveraging Enabling Technology

1. *COVID-19: Longer Term Impact on Internal Audit* (Lake Mary, FL: The Institute of Internal Auditors, 2020).
2. *How Audit Departments Deliver Business Value Through Digital Transformation*, AuditBoard, 2020.
3. *State of the Internal Audit Profession*, PwC, 2019.
4. *What is Agile Auditing? The Benefits of Taking Your Audit Team Agile*, AuditBoard, 2020.
5. *State of the Internal Audit Profession*, PwC, 2019.
6. *Blockchain Technology and Its Potential Impact on the Audit and Assurance Profession*, Deloitte Development LLC., 2017.
7. *Gartner Glossary*, Integrated Risk Management (IRM), 2020.

CHAPTER 7
Agents of Change Aren't Secret Agents

1. *OnRisk 2021: A Guide to Understanding, Aligning, and Optimizing Risk* (Lake Mary, FL: The Institute of Internal Auditors, 2020).
2. Ibid.
3. Ibid.
4. Ibid.
5. Ibid.
6. Ibid.
7. Influence at Work, *Principles of Persuasion*, https://www.influenceatwork.com/principles-of-persuasion/, Tempe, AZ. Accessed Oct. 9, 2020.
8. TVA Office of Inspector General, Semiannual Report of the Office of Inspector General April 1, 2001 – September 30, 2001, Issued October 31, 2001. Accessed at: https://oig.tva.gov/reports/semi31.pdf
9. Ibid.
10. N. Chhaya, "How to Know If Your Humility Has Gone Too Far," *Forbes* (May 7, 2020).
11. K. Albrecht, PhD, BrainSnacks, "The Paradoxical Power of Humility: Why humility is underrated and misunderstood," Jan. 8, 2015.
12. Ibid.
13. Richard F. Chambers, *Trusted Advisors: Key Attributes of Outstanding Internal Auditors* (Lake Mary, FL: Internal Audit Foundation, 2017), 132.

CHAPTER 8
Business Acumen

1. Brian Hill, "What Is a Strong General Business Acumen?" Chron. Lynda Moultry Belcher, "Advantages and Disadvantages of Technology Advances," Chron.
2. Dr. Raymond R. Reilly and Dr. Gregory P. Reilly, "Building Business Acumen," *HR West* (December 2009).
3. R. Brodo, "Powerful Business Acumen Skills - 5 Critical Elements," *Advantexe, the power of practice*, https://www.advantexe.com/blog/business-acumen-skills-5-most-important-elements-of-a-learning-journey, Nov. 16, 2015.
4. O. Casselle, "Jobs of the Future Will Require More Technology Acumen," https://www.digitaladventures.com/news/2018/2/24/jobs-of-the-future-will-require-more-technology-acumen, 2018.
5. "Workplace Loyalties Change, but the Value of Mentoring Doesn't," *Knowledge at Wharton* podcast, Wharton School of Management, University of Pennsylvania, 2007.
6. Ibid.
7. Lillian T. Eby, Marcus M. Butts, Jaime Durley, and Belle Rose Ragins, "Are bad experiences stronger than good ones in mentoring relationships? Evidence from the protégé and mentor perspective," *Journal of Vocational Behavior* (2010).
8. Richard F. Chambers, *Trusted Advisors: Key Attributes of Outstanding Internal Auditors* (Lake Mary, FL: Internal Audit Foundation, 2017).
9. Richard F. Chambers, *The Speed of Risk: Lessons Learned on the Audit Trail*, 2nd Edition (Lake Mary, FL: Internal Audit Foundation, 2019).

CHAPTER 9
The Strategic Internal Auditor

1. Accessed at: https://na.theiia.org/translations/PublicDocuments/GPI-Elevating-Internal-Audits-Strategic-Impact-English.pdf
2. Paloma Cantero-Gomez, "The Seven Critical Skills of Successful Strategic Thinkers," *Forbes* (Feb. 5, 2019). Accessed at: https://www.forbes.com/sites/palomacantero-gomez/2019/02/05/the-7-critical-skills-of-successful-strategic-thinkers/?sh=38a455e6656b
3. Ibid.
4. Ibid.
5. Ibid.
6. Ibid.
7. Richard F. Chambers, *Trusted Advisors: Key Attributes of Outstanding Internal Auditors* (Lake Mary, FL: Internal Audit Foundation, 2017).
8. "The Seven Critical Skills of Successful Strategic Thinkers."
9. Ibid.
10. Ibid.
11. *Trusted Advisors: Key Attributes of Outstanding Internal Auditors.*
12. Brainzooming, "6 Characteristics of Strategic Thinking Skills vs. Tactical Thinking," Apr. 22, 2015. Accessed at: https://brainzooming.com/6-characteristics-of-strategic-thinking-skills/24101/
13. Ibid.
14. "Thinking big with business transformation Six keys to unlocking breakthrough value," Deloitte. Accessed at: https://www2.deloitte.com/content/dam/Deloitte/us/Documents/process-and-operations/us-sdt-think-big-business-transformation.pdf
15. Ibid.

CHAPTER 10
On Being Relationship Centric

1. Elaine Houston, "The Importance of Positive Relationships in the Workplace," *PositivePsychology.com* (2020), https://positivepsychology.com/positive-relationships-workplace/
2. Ibid.
3. "Relationship Building Skills: Definitions and Examples," *Indeed.com* (2020), https://www.indeed.com/career-advice/career-development/relationship-building-skills
4. Richard F. Chambers, *The Speed of Risk: Lessons Learned on the Audit Trail*, 2nd Edition (Lake Mary, FL: Internal Audit Foundation, 2019).
5. Richard F. Chambers, Charles B. Eldridge, Paula Park, and Ellen P. Williams, "The relationship advantage: Maximizing chief audit executive success," March 2011, http://www.kornferry.com/ institute/317-the-relationship-advantage-maximizing-chief-auditexecutive-success (accessed November 18, 2016).
6. "How to Know You Are a Change Agent," NOVARETE, https://novarete.com/how-to-know-you-are-a-change-agent/#:~:text=A%20Change%20Agent%20is%20essentially,such%20as%20a%20consultant%20or

7. "Qualities of Effective Change Agents," Michigan State University, 2019, https://www.michiganstateuniversityonline.com/resources/leadership/qualities-of-effective-change-agents/
8. "Seven Essential Traits of a Change Agent," Enclaria, 2019, https://www.enclaria.com/2019/02/05/seven-essential-traits-of-a-change-agent/
9. "Qualities of Effective Change Agents."
10. Fred C. Lunenberg, "Managing Change: The Role of the Change Agent," *International Journal of Management, Business, and Administration*, Volume 13, Number 1, Sam Houston State University (2010).
11. Chrissy Scivicque, "How to Be Proactive at Work: My 5 Step System," *eatyourcareer.com*, 2010, https://eatyourcareer.com/2010/08/how-be-proactive-at-work-step-system/

CHAPTER 11
The Innovative Mindset

1. Jay Sullivan, "Three Steps To Developing An Innovative Instinct — And The Questions To Ask Yourself To Get There," *Forbes* (2018).
2. Richard F. Chambers, *Trusted Advisors: Key Attributes of Outstanding Internal Auditors* (Lake Mary, FL: Internal Audit Foundation, 2017).
3. Ibid.
4. Mikael E. Björling, "5 key steps to creating an innovation mindset," *Ericsson Networked Society Lab* (2018), https://www.ericsson.com/en/blog/2018/5/5-key-steps-to-creating-an-innovation-mindset
5. Ibid.
6. Ibid.
7. Daniel Burrus, "Failing is learning: Fail fast to learn faster," *BBN Times*, https://www.bbntimes.com/companies/failing-is-learning-fail-fast-to-learn-faster
8. Ibid.
9. "COVID-19 and the future of business: Executive epiphanies reveal post-pandemic opportunities," *IBM Institute for Business Value*, 2020.
10. Ibid.

CONCLUSION
Agents of the Future

1. "How to Inspire Change in the Workplace: 10 Ways to Be a Powerful Voice of Change (Even When It Feels Impossible)," Inspiring Leadership Now, 2020, https://www.inspiringleadershipnow.com/how-to-inspire-change-workplace/
2. Russell A. Jackson, "Emerging Leaders," *Internal Auditor* (2020).